trademark TM
CORPORATE PROMOTIONS

BUSINESS GIFTS

AWARDS

PROMOTIONAL PRODUCTS

IMPRINTED APPAREL

AD SPECIALTIES

FOOD GIFTS

TCHOTCHKES

18 Lois Street

Norwalk, CT 06851

Toll-Free: 866.2IMPRINT

phone: 203.487.6009

fax: 203.406.9556

August, 2010

As a valued customer and loyal friend of the *Trademark* team, please accept this book with our best wishes and thanks for your continuing support.

You now have in your hands a truly unique, limited edition, one-of-a-kind book. You might ask, out of the many options to choose from, "why this gift?" I selected this book for the message it conveys - we are survivors. We must pick ourselves up and go forward stronger than we were before when adversity hits. As you will see, that's what happened on "Black Saturday."

In addition:

1. I personally know families who saw the flames – they were *that* close.
2. It made me conscious of my many blessings – among them are customers like you!
3. It made me think of survival – none of us are immune from the impact of possible financial, personal, terrorism, or natural disasters.
4. Many businesses and persons we know were impacted by the recent recessionary times. You and I are survivors and it's our responsibility to take steps to learn from the past in view of a stronger future.

Also, I personally know the team that made this book happen. They assembled a group of "strictly volunteers" who put in over four thousand hours to produce this book and to memorialize this event. They then sold tens of thousands of copies all over Australia and donated 100% of the profits to the Central Fire Authority and Red Cross relief effort there. In the same charitable spirit, the licensee in North America is donating 100% of their profits from sales of the book to charity. I really like that! It's a cause I'm glad to support.

Everything considered, I thought it was something truly very special and I wanted you to have it. This may be available in bookstores in the near future, but for now it's just for a few of us! Please enjoy it. We at *Trademark Corporate Promotions* truly appreciate you as a customer and value your loyalty. We look forward to meriting your ongoing support. If you are interested in purchasing *FIRESTORM*, or another publication, with your corporate application, please don't hesitate to give us call!

Sincerely,

Jim Pontefract

FIRESTORM

Photo: Jason South

7TH FEBRUARY 2009
BLACK SATURDAY'S
TRAGEDY

100% of the profits from the sales of this book will be donated to individual CFA stations for essential equipment purchases.

Did you know that the CFA lost seven fire trucks to February's fires? These expensive vehicles and other fire fighting equipment will be extremely costly and difficult for many stations to replace. Glenvale School Lilydale and Berwick campuses have decided to do what we can to help this invaluable volunteer firefighting force recover. This book has been designed as a means of raising funds for needy CFA stations in the affected areas where money will be donated to specific equipment procurement projects.

Published: 2009 (First Edition)
Compiled by a Committee of Parents & Friends of Glenvale School
(Lilydale & Berwick Campuses).
© 2009 Glenvale School Lilydale
PO Box 505 Lilydale, Victoria 3140
Published by: Glenvale School Lilydale
Designed by: Brad Maxwell, maxwellsmartdesign
Printed & bound by: McPherson's Printing Group
Promoted & Distributed by: Dennis Jones & Associates Pty Ltd
The publishers have made every effort to ensure the accuracy and currency of material supplied within its pages. No claims will be recognised for errors or omissions of material supplied or collected or for information that may be incorrect or outdated.

Publisher's note
FIRESTORM was born in concept as a memento book that would help meet the huge public thirst for information on the greatest natural disaster that has ever struck our country. We wanted it to be more than just another pictorial on Australian bushfire.

This was an extraordinary event and we wanted to create an extraordinary book. The total land size burnt on Black Saturday was equivalent to Melbourne and Sydney's metropolitan areas combined. That's approximately 352,000 hectares of land devoured, with the majority in just 12 hours - 29,333 hectares an hour!

The community was abuzz with stories from the thousands of Victorians affected directly by these fires. Incredible stories. The press reported brief snippets of accounts from survivors. We decided that what would make our book interesting, would be to include some real stories from real people that would help readers understand, empathise and share this awful tragedy.

Stories that would open our eyes as to what our fellow Australians experienced and endured in the teeth of that mighty inferno.

We set out approaching persons mentioned in the press, persons we knew from the affected areas, and the emergency organisations involved in the fire fight. And the stories came in thick and fast! We were overwhelmed by the response. People wanting to share, people wanting to talk, people wanting to let Australia know about the intensity and drama of that historic day. Persons sharing graphic images, videos and mobile phone snaps of a fiery fury of flame and devastating destruction. And so this book came together very quickly, very spontaneously, capturing very genuinely the real inside story about Black Saturday. The story everyone wants to know!

FIRESTORM

FROM THE TIME THE FIRE STRUCK IT ONLY TOOK

15 MINUTES

TO DESTROY EVERYTHING WE HAD

This account of Peter Brown and family shows the intensity and the speed of the fire, which caught many in an extremely vulnerable situation. In many cases the escape route was cut off as a result of the ferocity of the fire. Peter said, "By 3:00pm the fire was still 30 kilometres away but moving fast in our direction. Our decision was to stay and defend. Buckets were filled, fire fighting pumps primed, ladders placed in strategic positions - ready as we could possibly be". At 4:00pm Peter was not too concerned about the fire but had all his plans in place. However, just 55 minutes later, the Brown family was surrounded in flames with their only refuge being the swimming pool. "I could hear a significant roar over the noise of the tractor, it sounded like a low flying jet coming up the valley. As the firefront bore down on us we sheltered under soaking blankets in our swimming pool - with a camera. The pictures tell our story..."

WIND, FLAMES, DEAFENING
ROAR, CHAOS, TERROR....
THE FIREFRONT HIT US!

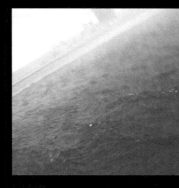

THE FIREFRONT PASSING THROUGH. POOL WATER BECOMES INCREDIBLY CHOPPY.

CROWN FIRE TAKES OUT UPPER BRANCHES AND LEAVES.

THE FRONT HAS PAST BUT THE HOUSE IS UNDER EMBER ATTACK! SMALL PLANTS IN FRONT OF THE HOUSE ARE ON FIRE.

WE HURRIEDLY GET OUT OF THE POOL TO FIGHT THE SPOT FIRES ON THE HOUSE. FIND PUMPS DISABLED FROM HEAT OF FIRE, USE BUCKETS.

A SPOT FIRE TAKES HOLDS ON THE UPPER DECK - NOTE THE LADDER IN PLACE TO TRY FIGHT THE FLAMES.

EMBERS HAVE ENTERED HOUSE, FIRE CANNOT BE CONTROLLED. WE RE-ENTER SWIMMING POOL IN DESPAIR.

THE FIRE TAKES HOLD IN THE UPPER STOREY AS WE COWER IN THE POOL.

6:02PM:
THE WIND SCREAMS, THE FIRE ROARS!

6:03PM:
THE FIRE SPREADS INCREDIBLY FAST THROUGH THE TOP STOREY.

6:03PM:
THE GUM TREE SUDDENLY EXPLODES INTO FLAMES.

6:03PM:
OUR HOME... ALL WE CAN SEE IS FLAME

6:04PM:
HEAT AND SMOKE INTENSE. WILL WE SURVIVE?

6:05PM:
EVERYTHING WE OWN IS BEING DEVOURED IN FRONT OF OUR EYES... IN JUST 15 MINUTES!

6:06PM:
FIONA IS HAVING TROUBLE BREATHING, WE DUCK DOWN IN WATER AND CONTINUE TO BREATH THROUGH WET BLANKET, CAMERA DAMAGED BY WATER AND CEASES OPERATION.

NEXT DAY:
A PICTURE OF THE AFTERMATH FROM THE SAME POSITION IN OUR POOL.

A MONSTER IS
BORN

LOCALS IN THE DISTRICT OF KILMORE HAVE CONCLUSIVELY AGREED ON THE LOCATION WHERE THEY SAY THE FIRE STARTED. AT ABOUT 11:20 AM ON SATURDAY 7TH FEBRUARY 2009 ON A WINDY HILLTOP ABOVE SAUNDERS ROAD IN KILMORE EAST, SMOKE AND FLAMES WERE SEEN IN A PADDOCK OF DRY GRASS. FIRE TRUCKS WERE CALLED BY SEVERAL LOCALS BUT IN NO TIME THE FIRE HAD JUMPED CONTAINMENT LINES AND BROKEN THROUGH EVERY BARRIER.

A MONSTER WAS BORN AND ITS GROWTH WAS UNCHECKED!

A howling north wind pushed the blaze through Wandong to St Andrews on the outskirts of Melbourne's northern bushy fringe. This is an area chosen by many for its tranquil lifestyle properties and easy living conditions, close enough to enjoy city benefits, yet far enough away to avoid the city rush. This band of fire then blasted right across the north of Melbourne's mountain ranges, through valleys, pastures and forests, down into the Yarra Glen regions renowned for their picturesque vineyards, some 50 kilometres from the fire's birthplace. A south-westerly wind change, instead of cooling the air, only served to multiply the areas under fire attack as the flank became a massive firefront. It devoured huge tracts of bush with total disregard for townships that stood innocently in its pathway.

Numerous locations were gruesomely savaged in the fire's pathway as it spread its tentacles through the Kinglake and Strathewen townships in fireball attacks which were fueled by the eucalypt vapour of gum trees exploding well ahead of the firefront.

DISASTER IN THE MAKING!

This disaster, encouraged by the lead up of harsh drought conditions, hurricane force winds and record temperatures after a prolonged heat wave, then became the deadly Black Saturday bushfires. Fires were so hot that up to 80,000 kilowatts of heat per metre were expelled as the fires raged that day. A senior university lecturer, Dr. Kevin Tolhurst, was reported as saying; "This was equivalent to about 1500 atomic bombs landing on Hiroshima."

Victoria, was unfortunately ideally placed for bad bushfires due to its climate, vegetation, topography and the extremely hot dry wind blowing down from the north in the continent's centre. These conditions were typical of other Australian bushfires known as Black Friday in 1939 and Ash Wednesday in 1983. The firestorm started in ideal terrain for fast fire-spread, in the undulating hills of the Central Highlands. It spread incredibly quickly up these slopes, literally doubling in speed. The effect of the hills creates a swirling wind pattern making fighting the fire almost unpredictable. Long distance forward spotting of the fires meant embers the size of footballs, along with burning branches, were thrown up to 15 kilometres ahead of the firefront. This made it impossible to control the fire in its early stages.

In a short space of time this small fire became an uncontrollable inferno that was unable to be stopped, even with air attack, which served mainly to save lives and homes rather than checking the progress of the bushfire.

0.1 FIREFIGHTERS RACE TO SAFEGUARD THE TOWNSHIP OF KILMORE.

0.2 PRINCESS ANNE MEETS FIREFIGHTERS IN WANDONG WHERE SHE TOURED THE CFA STATION, WANDONG PRIMARY SCHOOL AND THE RELIEF CENTRE.

0.3 ONLY A FEW BUILDINGS SURVIVED THE FEROCITY OF THE BLAZE.

0.4 FIREMEN DO ALL THEY CAN AS ANOTHER PROPERTY IS DESTROYED.

KILMORE EAST
WANDONG

Broadford

Humevale Rd

WANDONG RESERVOIR
TURNOFF 300m

Broadford Kilmore Rd

Hume Fwy

KILMORE EAST

KILMORE

Hume Fwy

Northern Hwy

WANDONG

MELBOURNE 50KM

SANDRA LACKAS

Wandong

TRAPPED IN THE
INFERNO

STEVE LACKAS, A JET SPRINTBOAT RACER, WAS A "CHEEKY AUSSIE LARRIKIN WHO LOVED TO STIR PEOPLE UP, EVEN IF HE DIDN'T KNOW THEM," SAYS HIS WIFE SANDRA. ALTHOUGH HE WAS ALWAYS PLAYING PRACTICAL JOKES ON PEOPLE, HE HAD A HEART OF GOLD, AND WOULD ALWAYS BE READY TO HELP ANYONE IN NEED. EVEN IF SOMEONE NEEDED A LOAN OR A GIFT, HE WOULD OFFER IT WITHOUT EXPECTING ANY FAVOURS IN RETURN.

Steve's passion for jet sprintboats was his life, and he was incredibly supportive of Sandra, and their son Bailey's love for ponies as well.

But on Saturday 7th of February, Steve perished just seconds before he was to make his dash for safety.

Steve was ready to escape, when he was overcome by flames in the sunroom of his house, only a metre from the back door. His coaster bus was waiting nearby with the engine idling. Only minutes earlier, he was on the phone to his wife and friends frantically describing the fire, as it was attacking the house. He said "I've got to go! I've got to go!" He then ran back into the house to grab a few more items before his dash for safety.

Steve was wearing his fire retardant racing suit, in the hope of bravely beating the flames. He had previously connected his jet sprintboat to the coaster bus, and filled the bus with some belongings. Sandra and Bailey had already gone down the mountain with the horses, but he had decided to wait back and try to save the house he had built. His decision to stay and defend the house proved to be fatal, as the blast of the fire destroyed everything in its path.

THE KEYS WERE IN THE
IGNITION WITH THE MOTOR RUNNING!

The keys were in the ignition of the bus with the motor running, but his safety route was cut off before he even got back to the vehicle. Ironically, only 30 metres away from where Steve was cruelly struck down, the vehicle was untouched by the inferno. Sandra is devastated by the tragedy, but is working with the comfort of her son, and help of family members to re-build their shattered lives. Steve is very, very sadly missed by Sandra and Bailey, who will always carry fond memories of him in their hearts.

Doomed gum trees make a desperate appeal to a lone fire truck in tinder dry conditions.

Photo: HWT

Photo: HWT

Broadford
VIA ALTERNATIVE
ROUTE
THIS EXIT

TAKING
REFUGE

WHITTLESEA, NORMALLY A QUIET TOWNSHIP AT THE EDGE OF MELBOURNE'S NORTHERN SPRAWL, HAD THE FIRES PASS BY THE FRINGE OF THE TOWNSHIP ON SATURDAY 7TH FEBRUARY AS IT SWEPT THROUGH TO ARTHURS CREEK AND HUMEVALE.

The area is noted for its laidback casual lifestyle and the many rural properties and horse ranches that abound through this undulating countryside situated east of the Hume Highway on the outskirts of Melbourne. Whittlesea became a major evacuation and emergency co-ordination centre for the area where thousands of people gathered for help and assistance.

Photo: HWT

0.1 CREATION HOLDS ITS BREATH AS DESTRUCTION LOOMS.

0.2 EMERGENCY SERVICES ARE AT BREAKING POINT AS SOS CALLS FLOOD IN.

0.3 RELATIVES CHECK THE NOTICE BOARD AT THE EVACUATION CENTRE, FOR NOTES FROM LOVED ONES.

0.4 LIKE A MENACING NIGHTMARE, THE FIRE ILLUMINATES THE HORIZON.

WHITTLESEA, HUMEVALE
ARTHURS CREEK

HUMEVALE

Whittlesea Yea Rd

WHITTLESEA

Grants Rd

MELBOURNE 45KM

Donnybrook Rd

Plenty Rd

Ridge Rd

ARTHURS CREEK

Bridge Inn Rd

The rolling hills of the Kinglake area could easily have been mistaken for a green carpeted mound rising out of the bushy outreaches of the northern extremities of Melbourne. There is a winding road that climbs the hills from the lower reaches of leafy St. Andrews, up the western face of the mountain, before crossing through a gap in the ridge to the eastern side of the crest, and into the quaint township of Kinglake. Houses can be seen dotted along the road as it approaches Kinglake tucked into the side of the hill like cozy sheltered hideaways, and hemmed in by giant gum trees in ferny backdrops. These beautiful rolling hills, just a stone's throw from the convenience of Melbourne, were like a magnet for people of all walks of life.

This picturesque community was caught unawares by a fire that went faster than vehicles and jumped gullies and ridges in its all-destructive pathway.

LIFE AFTER THE FIRE...

All that is left of a once beautiful landscape is the charred blackened tree trunks standing like motionless sentries in the grey surrounds. The fire seemingly froze the landscape as it roared through the hills, sucking all traces of moisture from the branches and trunks, and eradicating all traces of life from the bushy countryside. The endless kilometres of grotesque and lifeless trunks extend like a graveyard as far as the eye can see, down valleys, over hills and mountains, whilst a solitary twisting road clings to the edge of the mountain face. Several of the original buildings in the main street remain untouched, whilst other properties were wiped out and now have only basic temporary accommodation and makeshift shelters, telling a story of a fire that was unpredictable in its attack.

The community spirit of people reaching out to others in need shows clearly with the signs of "Free Food – Take What You Need" and the smell of sausages, onion and burgers filtering through the relief centres, which are buzzing with volunteers anxious to help the victims rebuild their shattered lives. These relief centres have been flooded with vast quantities of food, clothing, workshop items and toys for children in a generous spirit that has been truly overwhelming.

0.1 A bird flees for its life as hell fire looms.
0.2 Firefighters extinguish all traces of smouldering embers.

0.1

0.2

Photo: Craig Abraham

JASON LYNN

Kinglake

ESCAPE FROM
DEATH'S DOOR

Kinglake West was one of the areas that was destroyed by fire on Black Saturday 7th February 2009. As the terrible bushfires of north-west Melbourne closed in on Kinglake West, Jason Lynn had made the decision to stay and protect their property. How he emerged alive from a hell-fire onslaught to rejoin his wife and two children is beyond comprehension, but he did, and this is Jason's experience on that terrible day of suffering.

The fires have taken an obvious toll on the 35 year old's body, and the feelings that have burdened him recently, and the battle to recover after his survival, make it even more difficult to tell his story, especially when so many of his near neighbours didn't make it.

"I am not a hero," he says, "I did what I thought best on the day. The horror of that day will leave both physical and psychological scars on many, many persons and their properties for years to come."

A RECIPE FOR DISASTER!

That morning Jason noticed clouds of smoke high in the northern sky, a result of bushfires that had been burning throughout several parts of Victoria for several weeks after a long dry spell had left the state tinder dry. Saturday 7th of February was forecast to be the worst day in Victoria's history for bushfire danger and was actually stated by some as being the hottest place on earth that day. Combined with expected winds of up to 100 kilometres per hour, it was a recipe for disaster …and Disaster came!

Jason, his wife Ruth, and two children, Joshua 5 and Julia 3, lived on their 72 hectare Kinglake West property on the crest of a hill in a wooded belt of farmland where he kept a few cattle on his lifestyle hobby farm. Their cedar home with several out-buildings was surrounded by abundant natural wildlife, including kangaroos, wallabies and birdlife, and was a real taste of country life on the city fringe.

Jason had built a large dam and installed a pump with a 2 inch underground ring main that supplied water for three separate fire hoses strategically placed round the house and one in the wood shed. Two 35,000 litre water tanks were also part of his CFA approved fire plan. A sprinkler system around the eaves of the house was backed up by a generator connected to a pump on a water bore. Jason felt confident the house was well protected.

JASON HAD DECIDED TO STAY AND DEFEND!

But this was to be no ordinary fire. With virtually no warning for the area it was a matter of following survival instincts and bushfire training.

Ruth was involved in the local fire guard and the emergency plan was that they would be notified if fire action was required. There was no notification that day. It came so fast and was so fierce. They had planned their fire escape many times and the decision was made for Ruth to go with the kids. Jason had decided determinedly to stay and defend. The quietly spoken father of two small children was resolute to save their home. Whilst Ruth was rushing to load the car with the kids and a few of their possessions, Jason took an urgent phone call at about 4.00pm from his boss Ziad, an electrical contractor, who had been watching the staggering pace the raging fires were progressing through nearby Mount Disappointment.

Ziad had to yell in his phone over the wind noise to Jason. "Get out now! This is an animal of a fire that's devouring everything in its path." But Jason was definite; he had decided to stay.

As Ruth drove off into the wild winds, Jason prepared for the worst. He ran to the dam, primed the pump and started the generator on the bore pump that connected the sprinklers attached to the eaves of his house. Whilst running to ensure everything was operating correctly, he was yelled at from a passing CFA vehicle that stopped suddenly out the front – "What are you doing?"

"I'm staying – how long till it's here"?

"Three to five minutes," was the hasty reply, before speeding off down the dust road towards the main Whittlesea Kinglake Road.

JASON FELT ALONE!

Jason felt alone, and the eerie sky was changing to dark orange as the smoke clouds billowed like a natural signal light of warning. Then, an unusual, sudden calm in the wind became evident, giving a false sense of security as the front of the firestorm approached the property.

Ruth and the children had turned south towards Ziad's house in Whittlesea, not realizing the fire was intensifying in that area, and columns of cars were blocking the road. The visibility was down to almost nil, and the intense smoke was swirling overhead as Ruth retraced their path, and actually drove past the end of her street in their flight to the township of Yea some 50 kilometres to the north. This was to prove a life- saving decision for Ruth and the children, as many vehicles perished on other nearby roads that afternoon.

I AM NOT A HERO, I DID WHAT I THOUGHT BEST ON THE DAY

At about 4:30pm the flames appeared in the treetops over the Kinglake property, the wind started to howl again, but this time with the roar of a jet plane overhead. Everything started lighting up, a house over the road exploded in fire and a mob of terrified horses galloped directly into the firefront. Jason was putting out fires all around the house, and thought he was coping well, when Coombs Rd became enveloped in a tornado-like firestorm. He could see the swirling fires whipping the trees into a frenzy, as the blackened sky silhouetted the inferno that was engulfing everything in its path. It was absolutely terrifying to witness. The hay shed and stables exploded into flames and he knew it was impossible to save them with the hundreds of hay bales that were fueling the flames.

EUCALYPT VAPOUR IGNITED INTO A HUGE BALL OF SPITTING FLAMES

Jason kept hosing the house in an effort to save his life dream and keep a roof over the family. A hurricane of embers, some as big as a fist, were raining against the house as Jason cowered behind the fire hose. His heavy woollen jacket, overalls, woollen socks, boots, leather gloves and wide brimmed leather hat were his only protection against the radiant heat that was sapping his energy. A paper breathing mask offered some protection from the smoke and blistering heat, but not nearly enough. The oxygen was depleting and it was becoming difficult to breathe. "I could see the eucalypt vapour hovering over the gum trees," said Jason when suddenly... it ignited into a huge ball of spitting flames that hurled itself 20 metres or more ahead of the fire. These fire balls happened many times as the fires took hold of groups of gum trees. The fire hose was my only defence, but suddenly the water stopped. I ran towards the dam to realise my biggest fear, the dam pump was ablaze, caused by ember attack. Back at the house the sprinklers stopped working, as the generator also burst into flames.

Next, the open shed protecting the tipper and bobcat caught alight, which was adjacent to the hayshed. It was all Jason could do then to try and save the house with buckets of water. For the next exhausting ten minutes or so, he did everything he could to put out the growing army of flames licking at the house. They had a childrens' pool on the rear deck, and he kept running and filling a bucket from the pool and dousing flames wherever they appeared. Whilst doing this, Jason fell through the deck which was burning from underneath, and he realised he was losing the battle to save the house. He clambered to his feet and could hear the three dogs howling behind a shut gate that had burst into flames. After several attempts to beat the heat, he finally kicked in the burning gate. It fell apart allowing the dogs to escape into the darkness - an act of bravery that he could only have done for very close friends.

IN MINUTES THE WHOLE HOUSE WAS ENGULFED!

"I watched in horror as the house erupted into flames," said Jason, "and in minutes the whole house was engulfed. It seemed like a transparent house as the flames burnt the weatherboard cladding and ravaged through each room. I could see our queen-sized bed burning in the bedroom, and I could make out Julia's cot in the next room through the howling flames. It was like the death of the house, as it slowly sank to the ground. Everything was alight and the intensity of the flames stung my eyes and throat each time I looked at the tragic scene unfolding before me."

Next, Jason tried to save the Holden work ute. As the blistering heat made it impossible to sit inside the cab, Jason half hung out the door and managed to drive it into the big machinery shed some 30 metres away – his final retreat in a losing battle. This raging fight against time, and an inferno he had never witnessed before, culminated in defending the high walled metal shed that housed his speedway sprint car and the handmade tools his father had passed on to him prior to dying of cancer some years earlier.

Jason kept running to the dam forty metres away, bringing buckets of water back, climbing the ladder, and then emptying the 25 litre buckets down the walls of the shed. While standing on the roof of the shed, he heard a horn tooting amidst the roar of the fire. Jason realised that his wife's Toyota Forerunner which she had just washed in readiness for selling, had caught alight next to the shed and was blazing fiercely. He then witnessed the whole car suddenly explode in a ball of flames. As he was pouring water over the roof, he noticed the skylights had turned orange-red beneath him. The shed had ignited from the inside and suddenly the skylight roof sheeting blew out into the air nearly throwing Jason off the roof, and the flames were leaping through the skylight openings in a frenzied fire attack. The heat was unbearable and the lack of oxygen was forcing Jason to gasp for breath. It was then he then realised the ladder leaning against the shed had blown over in the wild wind and being too weak to jump the 5metre drop, he grabbed hold of the guttering, but it broke away from the roof. As it peeled off its mountings, it lowered him to the ground in a precarious procedure. Another prayer for help answered!

He leapt to his feet in desperation to get away from the furnace in the shed that was twisting the iron cladding into contorted shapes. The crackling, banging and pinging could be heard over the noise of the fire, as the beams gave way under the stress of the heat. Jason stooped as he made a crouched dash to get away from the last building he defended.

JASON RAN BLINDLY INTO A HALF-FALLEN WIRE FENCE

In his exhausted state Jason ran blindly into a half-fallen wire fence that entangled him. His brain numb with the pain, he couldn't think enough to back off and try again. For what seemed like an eternity he lay struggling to get over the seemingly impossible tangle of wire. He finally wrenched himself clear, and with his energy spent, he crawled over the blackened paddock. Every muscle in his body seemed cramped as if crying out subconsciously to stop and give up.

The dam is my only hope, thought Jason. The fire seemed more ferocious than ever and blue flashes of electrically charged lightning were shooting through the burning trees. "I can still see it etched into my memory, and I knew it was a phenomenon, even in my dimmed state of alertness," said Jason. Jason's jacket was smoldering and he pulled his leather hat hard down over his head in the blackness of the firestorm. The air was raining burning twigs, branches and embers and one ember actually burnt the inside of Jason's ear.

The phone rang during those agonising minutes and Jason mumbled into the phone. It was Jason's boss Ziad, on the other end;

"What are you doing Jason?"

"I'm trying to find the dam."

"Just get into the dam, don't stop till you find it!"

"Please tell my wife and kids, and my Mum that I love them. I think I'm going to die."

"No way, you'll make it to the dam, - keep going."

Ziad rushed to CFA headquarters in Whittlesea to tell the Officers, "There's a man in Kinglake West at 325 Coombs Rd who's trapped in the fire." The firemen confirmed the only right decision. "It's still too dangerous to get up there." At that time, the teenage daughter of Jason's church Pastor came into the station with trays of sandwiches for volunteers and listened to Ziad's pleas to help Jason.

She pricked up her ears and said, "I know that family, you mean Ruth and Jason." They were members of her father's church – Assembly of God Church.

JASON CRAWLED INTO THE DAM

After pleading with the CFA she ran to tell her father. Meanwhile, Jason had crawled in a half conscious daze until he'd located the slope of the dam. He then crawled down the embankment, and fearing he would drown, he had turned around and backed himself into the water leaving his head lying on the mud at the water's edge. The phone had rung just prior to entering the water and amazingly he had kept it clear of the water, whilst hardly conscious of the words he spoke as his phone lay against his ear.

He was shaking violently and breathing heavily whilst his church pastor prayed with him over the phone. Jason is unsure whether he remembers it, or just the fact he has been told since, that he was groaning, then silence, then mumbled whispers that could not be understood by those frantic friends that kept a prayerful vigil at the CFA station. Pastor Shane Lepp found it difficult to keep calm through the traumatic experience.

BARELY BREATHING IN AN UNCONSCIOUS STATE!

For two hours Jason lay at the dam's edge, shaking from exposure, unconscious and hardly breathing.

A CFA ute was finally able to stop at the property where the radio operator had told them of a man lying in a dam who was still alive.

A rigger's glove slapping his cheek, and a voice calling and calling him to wake up, was Jason's scant memory of his life-saver's arrival. Not having the strength to speak he was able to squeeze the hand that held his and a voice returned, "You have made it this far, you'll be alright mate." The volunteers lifted him out of the dam onto a blanket and carried him to the ute. They cradled him through paddocks as they cut fences and got through debris-scattered terrain to get him back to the Whittlesea showgrounds, where helicopters and ambulances were evacuating the wounded and screaming victims.

JASON WAS VOMITING MUD!

All this time Jason was convulsing and vomiting mud, which he had breathed in for so long whilst lying at the dam's edge.

For three days Jason recovered in hospital from burns, eye and respiratory problems. His airways were badly singed. Ruth and the children were reunited with Jason the night after the fire.

Thankfully the dogs were recovered at the Vet. They had fled to a neighbour's property (who died that terrible day). They had been brought to the vet, and were being kept in a cage with a tag on it – 'Owner deceased.' Jason said it was God's mercy that Ruth and all the children are together again, and the dogs once again roam the hilltop property. Together they have decided to rebuild their home and continue living on the property.

Photo: Angela Wylie

0.1 A grandmother provides reassurance in the remains of a Kinglake Church
0.2 Authorities attend to the grim task of recovering human remains

0.1

0.2

A 12-year old boy finds the remains of his BMX amongst the ruins of his house.

Photo: Jason South

68 elbourne B300 Yea 38

Ice Cold BEER
FINE WINES

VALLEY OF
DESTRUCTION

FIREFIGHTERS DESCRIBE THE TINY TOWNSHIP OF STRATHEWEN AS THE "VALLEY OF DEATH". IT HAD NO HOPE AND HAS BEEN ALMOST TOTALLY WIPED OFF THE MAP. DEATH'S CRUEL HAND STRUCK WITH BRUTAL FORCE. THE FIRE DIDN'T DISCRIMINATE BETWEEN THE YOUNG OR THE OLD, THE WELL PREPARED OR THE STRICKEN. THE IDENTITY OF THIS TOWNSHIP, TUCKED AWAY INTO THE VALLEY BENEATH THE RANGES OF KINGLAKE, HAS BEEN OBLITERATED IN A CRUEL TWIST OF FATE.

Photo: HWT

0.1 ANOTHER GRUESOME TRAGEDY WHICH DRAWS OUT SYMPATHY FOR FAMILY MEMBERS AFFECTED.

0.2 TREES EXPLODE CREATING UNSTOPPABLE FIREBALLS.

0.3 THE CRIPPLED REMAINS OF WHAT WAS ONCE A BEAUTIFUL MOUNTAIN TOP DWELLING.

0.4 EVEN THIS DUMP TRUCK COULD NOT WITHSTAND THE INTENSITY OF THE FIRE.

STRATHEWEN
ST ANDREWS

STRATHEWEN

MELBOURNE 35KM

Arthurs Creek

ST ANDREWS

Kinglake

Whittlesea-Kinglake Rd

Healesville-Kinglake Rd

Heidelberg Kinglake Rd

STRATHEWEN IS ACCESSED BY A LONG TWISTING ROAD THROUGH THICK BUSH. IT IS A REMOTE TOWNSHIP THAT IS SET IN UNDISTURBED PEACEFUL BLISS. FOUR WHEEL DRIVE TRACKS FREQUENTED BY OFF ROAD ENTHUSIASTS ABOUND IN THE AREA, BUT THERE IS ONLY ONE MAIN ROAD THAT LEADS INTO THE TOWN.

Apart from the fire station, which amazingly survived the scene of utter devastation, only the chimneys and charcoaled remains of the towns 40 houses are left. Each house has been reduced to just piles of twisted roofing sheets lying over the remnants of blackened bathtubs, and carcasses of metal fridges. Almost everything else was reduced to just ashes.

Only a few people stayed behind when the fires approached the township and many burnt out vehicles lying strewn along the roadside were a testament to the fire's ferocity. A bridge along the road of their only escape route was also damaged by fire, as the inferno thrust through the once pristine valley. Two burnt out shells of cars mark the panicked last minute decision of several residents, who would have realised only too late that they could not outrun this all engulfing firestorm.

One local man and his wife drove to the footy oval as the hell-fire bore down on them. When he found the gates locked, he ran into a nearby paddock and screamed at his wife to drive to a neighbour's house. She made it, but he didn't.

Another local, racehorse trainer Dennis McCrohan and wife Joy, lost 13 horses and many of their friends in Saturday's trail of destruction, but survived by fleeing to their dam after failing to save their house.

Dennis McCrohan has told reporters that he and his wife had defied advice at a fire briefing earlier in the year to jump into the dam, but had survived against all odds. "We tried to save the house, being well prepared with sprinklers and hoses and fought if off for an hour, but we had no hope. We gave up the fight when the tables and chairs inside the house caught alight."

The car was nearby, and we took woollen blankets, then ran for the car and drove down to the dam. We waited in the dam for three quarters of an hour. "We lost the lot – house, stables, sheds – everything's gone but we're alive," he said.

Many who were eager to survive amidst overwhelming odds had tried to outrun nature and persons who had gambled on a last minute dash to safety had been caught helplessly in the firestorm.

ST ANDREWS

St Andrews was originally known as Queenstown when it was part of the Caledonian goldfields and it abounded with alluvial gold in the Diamond Creek that runs through the centre of the little township.

One well known local, Reg Evans, 81 years old, died on Saturday fleeing the bushfires that engulfed his home. He had appeared in many films, and was well liked for his uncanny portrayal of the characters he played. He had roles in just about every Australian drama on TV, from Homicide to Blue Heelers and also films such as Mad Max.

Strathewen and nearby St. Andrews will carry the burden of their losses for years to come. Houses can be rebuilt and replaced, but the character and influence of friendly towns people have gone forever and will never be replaced.

Photo: Newspix

0.1 MOLTEN ALUMINIUM WHEEL — EVIDENCE OF THE INTENSE HEAT.

0.2 A HOUSE ONCE DEPICTING TRANQUILITY HAS BECOME VICTIM OF THE ROARING FIRE.

0.3 REALITY OF THE FIRE'S FORCE IS SHOWN IN THE REMAINS OF WHAT WAS ONCE A HOUSE.

0.4 THIS CAMPER VAN STOOD NO CHANCE AS THE FIRES TORE THROUGH.

A scorched and blackened landscape is testimony to the fires relentless power. 0.5

BUNKER
JIM!

JIM HAS LIVED A GOOD PART OF HIS LIFE IN THE ST. ANDREWS AREA. SIXTEEN YEARS AGO JIM BUILT HIS DREAM HOME ON HIS HEAVILY WOODED 87 ACRES ON A DIRT ROAD RUNNING BETWEEN ST. ANDREWS AND STRATHEWEN. LIVING THERE HAD MADE HIM REALISE THAT BUSHFIRES COULD HAPPEN AT ANY TIME AND SO HE PREPARED FOR THEM.

Six years before the 7th of February 2009, Jim prepared. He dug into the hill directly behind the house and built a fire proof bunker.

Jim and his family were up as usual on Saturday the 7th. They were aware it had been predicted to be a high fire danger day but they went about their usual Saturday morning routine. Jim went to work, as he had some international visitors who wanted to work this incredibly hot and windy day, and his wife had taken the children to their usual round of activities.

Jim finished up work just after mid-day, and then headed for his St. Andrews home. On the way to his house, Jim was alerted to fires burning in the Kilmore area and other areas closer to his home. His wife rang and questioned if he should be heading to the family home, but Jim assured her that everything was OK.

A SMALL SPOTFIRE HAD STARTED!

At about 4:00pm, as Jim approached his home, he came across a small spot fire that had been started by burning embers. He pulled up straight away and grabbed his mobile phone. Dialing '000' to call the emergency services, Jim experienced the frustration that many faced that day! He was given the ring around on the phone, but eventually got his message through that a fire had started in the St. Andrews area. Jim couldn't wait any longer, as he had his own house to worry about, so he accelerated fast up the dirt road heading for home, and he just hoped that the message would get help there quickly.

The heat was extreme, and the wind was blowing like a cyclone by the time he arrived home. Jim was really concerned, and could feel his adrenaline flowing. Things were getting worse and worse as he pulled out the fire pump and connected the hoses. He threw some important items, including the photo albums and computers, into the bunker. There was no time for anything else now, except to wait for the fire.

A NUCLEAR MUSHROOM CLOUD BUILDING UP IN THE SKY!

Jim watched the massive pillar of rising smoke from the Kilmore direction, and noticed it was obviously spreading rapidly. The smoke was billowing high into the air, and it looked like a nuclear mushroom cloud, building up in the sky! This could not be good, thought Jim. He was scanning the horizon intensely, and was well

This rare but horrifying sequence of photos is by Jim Baruta, who witnessed the onslaught of the firestorm on his property... and lived to tell the tale.

aware the fire was moving rapidly in his direction.

By 4:50pm, it was clear that the whole area was going to be under direct flame attack very shortly. This was not just a localized fire approaching, it was a wildfire inferno.

Within minutes, he could see the flames crashing through the trees on the hilltop several kilometres away. Jim did a quick calculation, and realised the fire would be on him in about ten minutes. It would have only been three or four minutes later when fires started breaking out all over the neighbour's paddock. "I could hear the cows mooing in panic, as the fire engulfed the paddock," he said. Suddenly, one of the neighbours' houses erupted into flames, and the fire roared over the tree tops, bursting from tree to tree, rising over twice the height of the surrounding bush as it swallowed every object in its pathway. By now, the fire was racing like an express train out of control, and the wind was swirling the blaze across the gully leading towards him. Jim realised that the fire was now about to close in on his own house.

ANOTHER NEIGHBOUR'S HOUSE ERUPTED INTO FLAMES!

Jim watched in horror, as another neighbour's house exploded into flame. "How are we going to get through this?" he said aloud, and several other exclamations rolled off his tongue. The fire was now thrusting towards him, devouring everything in its path.

Watching in horror, as the fire closed in on him from both sides, the extreme noise sounded like twelve jet planes landing on his house! Through all this, Jim had been videoing the unfolding hellfire, and what a video he took, as a great fiery wall headed his way.

Jim had built his bunker to withstand a bushfire, but could it withstand this monster, this mega-fire? It seemed like there was no escape. His driveway was right through the middle of this raging inferno, and the bunker would have to endure the ultimate test of survival, in the ensuing time ahead of him....

The fire had just covered about ten kilometres in about four minutes, and flames were eating into the edge of his property. The heat was intense and the wind was at gale force. The fire was sucking, sucking everything towards it! Jim could see the tall gum trees bending at incredible angles, being overcome by the fire's power as it accelerated towards him. "Here it comes!," Jim screamed, to anybody who cared to listen! He still held on, filming this monster, as the fire burst through the last line of trees and his driveway. The front of the property then disappeared in a fireball, which leapt up to one hundred metres into the air. The sky had turned from black to red, and back to black again, while the smoke came pouring in low, making it extremely hard to breathe.

Jim had prepared for this fire well in advance; he had put his thick leather clothing in the swimming pool to soak them thoroughly with water. He now sprinted around the edge of the house, grabbed a heavy wet sack from the pool, then ran onto the front lawn.

HIS LUNGS WERE BURNING WITH PAIN!

Beating at the grass flames, he soon realised that it was too much for him. Feeling like he had just run a marathon race, he was short of air, and his lungs were burning with pain. What's wrong with me, he thought, and then realised that the fire itself was consuming the very oxygen he was trying to breathe. Dropping the sack, Jim ran for the verandah again, and less than two seconds after he got there, the main firefront hit! With just enough time to step behind a brick pillar, allowing the main fury of the fire to pass

both sides of him, he distinctly remembers a screaming mass of burning debris, flying horizontally through the air. All hell had unleashed its wildest fury. Jim knew immediately, he couldn't stay a second longer where he was; the heat was extreme, and the wind was lifting him off his feet.

THE FIRE BURST OVER THE TOP OF THE BUNKER!

Jim knew he had to make it to the bunker. He walked down the verandah, knowing he couldn't run, in case he fell. Had he fallen, he would never have been able to get up again in that burning fury, and would have been consumed where he fell. Walking calmly with the fire at his back, he made it to the bunker. Slamming the door behind him, Jim could only wait, and hope he was going to make it through. The fire then burst over the top of the bunker. He watched it through a small hole in the wall. It reminded him of somebody outside with an oxy torch, trying to cut their way in. Every little crack and gap around the door, had fire licking through it. The bunker held him safe, the heat was intense, but he could still manage to breathe. Realizing time was limited, as the fire sucked the oxygen out of the bunker; Jim knew he couldn't stay there too long. He also realised he would lose his house, so after about 10 minutes he slowly opened the door and ventured out. What met his eye, made him catch his breath. Everything around him was burning, and all he could think of was to try and save his home. He reached for the fire hose, and started hosing the gas bottles that were venting gas. He feared the bottles would blow up, so standing behind a wall he sprayed them, to cool them as fast as he could. Suddenly, the water supply stopped. He raced to the tap, but noticed that the hoses had burst in the ground, cooked from the top down! Sprinting to his fire pump he started it first shot, then opened the throttle full bore, and set the pump in motion. Instantly, the draw pipe into the pump collapsed, and the water supply stopped! What now? How could he save his house? He quickly remembered the swimming pool, found a bucket, and started a four hour marathon fight against the aftermath of the fire. The verandahs were alight, and he needed the strength to save his home, and having endured the worst fire storm in Australia's history, he wasn't about to give up now! Well into the evening and through the night, Jim went backwards and forwards from the swimming pool to his precious house, until finally at about 3:00am in the morning, with eyes burning out of his head, satisfied he had won the war of saving his home for now, he collapsed in total exhaustion!

THE AFTERMATH!

The next day, he was up before sunrise, and all the time, the fire was lessening. Jim made contact with his wife again, and found that she couldn't get to him as the roads had been blocked by the authorities, as well as a huge amount of fallen trees. Jim got on a motor bike, and headed out to see if any neighbours needed help. The few living ones he found appeared to be all right, but they had lost their homes. He passed several cars and a van, and knew that any people inside would have perished. Nothing could have prepared him for this shocking experience. So many people had perished, after being trapped trying to flee the extreme wrath of the firestorm!

Two days later, Jim was reunited with his relieved wife and children.

For Jim, the experience felt like he had lived through hell, and come out the other side. All he had intended to do, was to take a video for his children to view, but instead he had created a video that would shock the world, with the extreme and immeasurable volume of flaming fury, that was thrown at mankind, on that terrible day . . . Black Saturday.

EVERYTHING AROUND HIM WAS BURNING APART FROM HIS HOUSE

0.1

Photo: Newspix

0.1 The immense strength of the firestorm is shown in what is left of this street sign. **0.2** The road winding from Melbourne to Kinglake becomes a moonscape. 0.2

FERN LANGMEAD

Strathewen

WE SURVIVED IN
THE DAM

WE SURVIVED IN THE DAM WITH A DEER AND KANGAROOS

It is now over two months since the greatest peacetime disaster in Australian history turned my world upside-down. Black Saturday is a name that hardly does justice to the day that is etched permanently into the minds of innocent victims. But I remember it as 'Hell on Earth'.

The bushfires that devastated Victoria on the 7 February, 2009, all but wiped our tiny little community of Strathewen, from the face of the planet.

For seven generations my family have lived and worked on the land in the Valley of Ewen, and in one horrific afternoon any trace of that past, that family history, was destroyed. In the space of a heartbeat, we lost everything.

THE SMOKE TURNED THE SUN BLOOD RED!

It was around 3:00 pm when the heavy cloud of smoke that was billowing in the sky started to drift closer to home. It hung thick in the air, and I was already finding it difficult to breathe. The hellish black cloud spread over the iconic Mount Sugarloaf like a warning that none of us heeded. The smoke turned the sun blood red, whilst casting an eerie golden glow over the landscape. At this point I was alone at home, unaware of the real danger looming just beyond the mountain.

When Dad, Nyall and Earle did return home, we still weren't sure that the fire was heading for us, but we put fire overalls on, grabbed our masks and gloves, and prepared ourselves for the worst, just in case it kept coming our way. Thankfully Mum had been in hospital overnight for chemo, and due to a high temperature was unable to return home that day as planned. Rikki and Mal had also left early with Aidan, just in case things turned nasty.

I had already opened all the gates to the property so that if the fire did come, the horses would be able to run to wherever they thought was the safest place to ride it out. It probably saved their lives.

Earle took the Australian flag down and put it in his fire overalls. If we were going to survive, so was the flag.

Our fire plan was prepared should we decide to stay and defend the property, and we executed the plan perfectly. No plan though, however perfect, could have stopped that humongous fire. I'd already packed some things ready to put in the car, but by this stage it was clearly too late to evacuate, and I came to the conclusion that there was no point putting everything in the car, because it would only burn in the fire anyway. I thought the house would be safer. How wrong I was! My car made it

out of there with barely a scratch. I kick myself everyday for that. Saving something would have made the other losses a little easier to bear.

I TURNED THE CARS AROUND READY FOR THE MAD DASH!

The smoke and embers hit us long before the fire did. The boys were trying frantically to stamp out any embers that came close to the house whilst Dad got the pumps ready, and I turned the cars around ready for the mad dash to the dam...... In case it came to that!

Dad got a call from work, saying that the fire had jumped containment lines in Humevale, and that it was heading straight for us. This was the first warning of the fire coming our way, and the only time we knew that we were in danger. Within two short minutes, the fire was on us. An uncontrollable wild animal of a fire, roaring like 50 jungle lions, suddenly confronted us.

WE WERE CORNERED!

The flames rose higher than the mature gums on the mountain, in a fire engine red tornado. Like the greatest nightmare of hell, the smoke turned day into night, and spot fires were igniting everywhere. Down the driveway and up the top of the hills on either side of us, it came rushing towards us. We were cornered. The wind was blowing with a hellish fury in all directions, and the heat was so intense we had to shield our faces to breathe.

We had no time to look for pets, neighbours, or even each other. We could only scream over the roar to get to the cars as there was no choice but to make a run for it. We could never defend ourselves with hoses and sprinklers against that nightmare inferno.

I heard Dad scream at us to get to the cars, so we ran screaming for Earle as we did, because he had made his way to the front of the house, and we couldn't see him anywhere. There was nothing we could do except try to save ourselves, and each other.

DAD WAS SCREAMING!

With pounding hearts we made our mad dash to the dam in the cars. Dad was screaming over the roar of the fire to slow down as I nearly ran up the back of Nyall. We drove into the paddock, then parked by the bank, and ran for the water, only stopping to remove our boots. We threw our wallets and phones onto the bank of the dam hoping they would be there if we survived, so we could call Mum and tell her we made it out of there . . .If we did!

We swam out towards the middle of the dam, taking our overalls on as we swam, because they were weighing us down. Nyall kept his on, but Earle turned his overalls into a floatation device. I remember panicking that the water would heat up, and that we would boil to death, but Dad reassured us the water was too deep. Fire was starting to burn all around us now, racing down the hill towards us. Earle was helping support Dad, as he isn't a strong swimmer, and he wasn't able to hold himself and Dad afloat for much longer.

WE WERE SHARING THE DAM WITH A FRIGHTENED DEER!

We decided to move closer to the edge where we could stand up, and shelter with the woollen blanket over our heads.

The boys and Dad got to the edge first, and by now we were sharing the dam with a frightened deer and some kangaroos. We were all finding comfort in the cool water. It was an amazing sight. Fire is the common dread of both man and beast alike, and every other fear recedes in the face of it.

Then the firefront hit……. I was still out in the water when the full force of the fire storm hit. Hot embers and black smoke attacked us with an unrelenting ferocity that is hard to put into words. I couldn't breathe. Every time I tried, I felt my lungs burning like crepe paper. I heard the others screaming my name out, but in the smoke it was difficult to see where I was. At this point I thought I was going to die.

THIS WAS HOW I WOULD DIE!

There were no ifs, buts or maybes. This was how I would die. At the age of 27, with an unfinished life, it was a fleeting thought, but it was there, and it was very real. Then I swam underwater, only coming up twice for the tiny bit of air that I could get before reaching the others. If they were any further away I don't think I would have made it. The blanket became my worst nightmare when the claustrophobia kicked in, but it saved our lives.

I WENT UNDER THE WATER EVERY 30 SECONDS

We spent two hours under that old woollen blanket, going under the water every thirty seconds or so to clear the smoke that had formed, and to put out the hot embers that stuck to the wool. After about an hour or so we were able to check what was happening around us, but then the wind would pick up and blow burning embers towards us again. We would then have to go back under the safety of the blanket. It was like a life support blanket that shielded us from the intensity of the heat and fiery embers.

I think the shock hit us eventually, because we all started making stupid jokes about needing a beer. The reassurance I got from the others, helped pull me through. I honestly think that if there had been one less of us, or one more, no one would have made it out of there alive.

Dad's car caught fire and we were so worried that it would explode that we moved along the dam a bit. Nyall got out and grabbed the phones and wallets just before they melted or caught fire.

I THOUGHT EVERYONE WE KNEW WAS DEAD!

All of a sudden it was daylight again. The smoke had lifted, and we assumed it was safe to come out of the blanket. Nyall tried to make a phone call, but with no reception he had to walk towards home to call out. I remember Dad and I were swearing at him and yelling because it was taking so long. Even then I didn't feel safe enough, and thought he might die trying to make a phone call.

I remember looking around at the total destruction that took only a short time to occur. It was as though a bomb had been dropped on us. There was nothing but blackness and red coals.

About an hour later, we risked going back up to the home to see if anything was left. The place was unrecognizable. There were fires still burning, but the house was gone. A pile of twisted roofing sheets lay on the glowing remains of our family home. The once towering gums were nothing but black sticks poking out of the once fertile earth. It looked like a war zone. Like something out of a disaster movie.

Nothing could have prepared us for that sight. Not even living through it.

My first priority was to see if any of the animals survived. I didn't hold much hope. As I made my way around Rikki's tank in the back yard I'd never felt such relief in my life as I turned the corner and saw my two horses standing there, frightened and shaking, but unharmed. I broke into tears as I thanked whoever was listening, that two of my babies had made it out alive. It was something at least.

RED HOT EMBERS WERE BURNING EVERYWHERE!.

The hills were black as night, and red hot embers of glowing timbers were burning everywhere. They looked like city lights.

All night was a paranoid waiting game. Whenever a tree would fall in the area it sounded like a bomb dropping and exploding with showers of fireworks spraying the air around it.

Rosemary's house was full of smoke and made it hard to breathe and every time I closed my eyes to try and sleep, I would see flames lighting up my vision. I was still so fearful that the fire would return whilst I was sleeping. We could hear the firefighters trying to clear the road with chainsaws and bobcats all night, and I kept wondering when they would get us out of here.

At 6:00 am whilst it was still dark outside, and the air was thick with smoke, we piled into my car and drove down the road. The road was barely a road anymore, just a dirt track with trees down everywhere. We passed several fire trucks, and some burnt out vehicles on the way, that hadn't made it out. It was still too dark to see anything clearly. An eerie light hung like a pall over the scene of destruction that heightened all our senses - especially fear! I remember a horse standing on the side of the road, stunned and unmoving, but alive. We passed the great community hall. Although no longer there, I know exactly where it once stood, and will again. We made our way to the Arthur's Creek fire station, unaware that the trauma was only just beginning.

The station became a meeting point for anyone who survived, and loved ones looking for their relatives. As every car pulled up, my heart would skip a beat, as I waited to see who else had survived. Eventually news of the less fortunate filtered in, and the number of close friends who lost their lives is still too unbearable to think of. The weeks that followed were just a blur.

We found our other two horses, alive and unharmed, but the dog and cat weren't so lucky. We found their remains when we could eventually get back to the property. It's a heavy weight on my heart that I carry with me every day.

After a month, the terrible fires of 'Black Saturday' are being forgotten by the general public, but for us involved it's only just the beginning. There is no closure, we have nothing to go back to, and the rebuilding process will take years. I find it hard to explain to people who weren't there, or who didn't lose everything that it's not as simple as going back to work and getting on with our lives. For some of us there is nothing to get on with. Jobs were lost, livelihoods ruined, and yes, it's been a month, but who says that grief should have a time limit?

MATERIALISTIC THINGS NO LONGER MATTER

For me, a career, money, and material things no longer matter. I had all that a lifetime's worth, and I lost it all in a heartbeat. What's more important is spending time with the people I love - my family and my friends. We will go back and start a new history in Strathewen. It will take a long time to forget the events of 'Black Saturday' and an even longer time to heal the scars. But I will make the most of my life. I have to, because it's all I have left…. And we will rebuild!

TONY IARAI

St Andrews

TONY IARAI'S EXPERIENCE
FLEEING THE FIRE

I gunned it down the road, slowing for a second to see my parents in-law racing out their driveway. "Follow me!" I yelled and we both took off like rockets down the dirt road. The flames were leaping up into the trees beside me and then began blowing across the road in front of us. We have to go through this I said to myself, so pushing the pedal to the metal, I flashed through the fire. Seconds later, my in-laws came through behind me. The smoke was blinding, but I knew the road well, so I pressed on! With everything burning, - houses, trees, fences, the lot, exploding into flames around me, I finally made it through to the main road. I pulled up to turn onto it and waited a minute for my father in-law to pull in behind me, but he didn't arrive!

"Oh no!" I thought. My heart sank as I racked my brains as to what I should do. Should I proceed on or return to find them? I thought quickly, "I can't leave them", so thankfully, in a split second decision, I turned the ute around and drove like a demon back into the flames. I rounded a corner and I could just make out their silhouette through the choking smoke and fire. There they were in the middle of the road, car on fire and about to explode. I did a screaming turn and came in beside them. They quickly scrambled into the ute, and we took off again. By now the embers were raining down hard on us, embers as big as dinner plates and fully alight were hammering the ute, and the trees were crashing down across the road behind us. Pity help anyone trying to make it out behind us! We reached the main road again and I floored it for St. Andrews township, leaving the fiery inferno behind us!

THIS WAS IT, HELL HAD COME TO EARTH.

POLICEMAN
SAVES GIRL

PAUL KEMEZYS

Strathewen

Police found themselves in life saving operations on Black Saturday as the day progressed from bad to worse, and the horror of fatalities took their toll. Whilst driving up a local road to check on a house under fire threat, we pulled alongside a DSE truck parked at the side of the road. We could see a little girl sitting on a blanket next to the dam with the DSE chaps sitting beside her. The DSE had found this girl in the dam and had just got her out. We called immediately for an ambulance, telling them it was life threatening, and I thought to myself- she's not going to make it! We sat down beside her and began pouring drinking water on her. Her legs were burnt, her arms were burnt, and we knew we just had to get an ambulance to her quickly.

We left her for a brief time with the DSE, while we went to check on the house further up the road to see if the owner had made it out. He obviously hadn't, and another few hundred metres up the road we came across three deceased people on the road. There was a van that was sort of parked diagonally across the road and it looked as if it had come down from the mountain. The driver had seen the fire coming towards him, and tried to turn around, but had got stuck. It appeared these people had then left their van and tried to make a run for it. They turned out to be the young girl's parents and a visitor, but we didn't know that at the time.

We then returned to the girl and called for an ambulance again asking where the closest one might be. The ambulance operator told us that the closest one was about 40 kilometres away, and they were not going to come because it was just too dangerous. So we thought, if they were not going to come to us, we would have to go to them. After clearing the back seat of our car, we put her in the back and radioed in saying, "Just let the Austin Hospital know that we've got a young girl on board with life threatening injuries. We're heading straight there, and she'll need life support immediately."

We headed off straight away and after about a ten or fifteen minute drive we came across our first ambulance, probably just by pure chance. They were parked on the side of the road, I don't know if they were lost or what, but we swapped roles and we got her out of our car into the ambulance. She was in a fairly bad way, as the ambulance driver then called a paramedics team, and they arrived and took her straight to hospital. She spent the next three weeks on life support in the Royal Children's Hospital.

Photo: Craig Ingram

How this house survived, is almost beyond human comprehension.

BUSH HAVEN
INCINERATED

THE TOURIST HAVEN OF STEELS CREEK, KNOWN FOR ITS WINERIES AND ORGANIC FARMS, WAS TORCHED ON BLACK SATURDAY AND LOST MANY OF ITS LOCAL RESIDENTS TO THE HORRIFIC FIRES. NEARBY HEALESVILLE, CHUM CREEK, DIXONS CREEK, AND YARRA GLEN WERE ALSO AFFECTED BY THE FIRES, BUT NONE OF THEM FELT THE FULL WRATH OF THE FIRE LIKE STEELS CREEK.

Steels Creek Road, a four kilometre stretch of road, had hardly any survivors to retell the horror that destroyed the close-knit community. More than 40 of the 50 homes on the road were obliterated in a fireball attack that raced up the valley in just a few minutes.

This quaint township, nestled into the foot of the Kinglake hills, just north of Yarra Glen, has been split apart by this natural disaster. Hardly a family in these stricken areas has not been affected by the death of a family member or friend. The losses and burnt possessions include family homes, rural businesses, vineyards, horses, cattle, and wildlife. The extent of wildlife losses will never be known and it may take years to re-establish to their former levels, but it is the human fatalities that cause untold sorrow and grief.

Residents in the town spoke of three children found huddled in a bathtub in the burnt out shell of one house. Another young man stayed to defend his parents dream home they had built for their retirement. When he realised the ferocity of the fire that was engulfing the valley, he phoned his parents to say "Goodbye!" That was the last time they would ever speak to him. Another local warned his neighbour of the impending fire that was bearing down on them. They packed their possessions beside each other in two adjacent driveways and as the first resident drove out, the last thing he saw of his neighbours was their car parked with the boot lid up in the driveway.

When he returned the next day, the neighbours' car was exactly where he last saw it, but now a burnt out shell, still with the boot up.

Some who fled their homes in an effort to escape, were cruelly cut down by the inferno after running off the smoke-filled roads into ditches.

Unable to escape by foot due to the radiant heat and flames, they lost their only avenue to safety once their vehicles became immobilized.

0.1 A FIREFIGHTER BATTLES TO STOP ANOTHER SPOT FIRE.

0.2 PICTURESQUE WINERIES WERE WIPED OUT, CAUSING HUGE FINANCIAL LOSS.

0.3 AN EERIE SILHOUETTE BEFORE DESTRUCTION.

0.4 NATURE BLATANTLY IGNORES THESE CRITICAL SIGNPOSTS.

Photo: HWT

STEELS CREEK, YARRA GLEN, COLDSTREAM
HEALESVILLE, CHUM CREEK

STEELS CREEK

MELBOURNE 37KM

CHUM CREEK

YARRA GLEN

HEALESVILLE

Maroondah Hwy

COLDSTREAM

CHARRED BODIES IDENTIFIABLE ONLY BY DNA PROCESSES

During the weeks following, teams of forensic investigators worked their way up every street identifying victims. The scale of destruction was almost impossible to comprehend. Police had the gruesome task of sifting through the ruins and debris to find charred bodies, identifiable only by DNA processes. This was an added horror for all those involved.

Photo: HWT

The only evidence of an occupant in some cars was the steel clip of the seat belt still fastened.

BRUNO CIMO
Castella

CASTELLA
SPLIT DOWN THE MIDDLE!

WHERE IS CASTELLA? IT'S A QUESTION I'VE BEEN ASKED OFTEN ENOUGH.

Let me start by saying that it is a place with somewhat of an identity crisis. Nestled in between Kinglake to the west, Toolangi to the east, and split down the middle by the Melba Hwy. Castella is in the shire of Murrindindi, yet it shares its postcode with Healesville and the shire of Yarra Ranges. In January 2006, as the fires crept ever closer from Glenburn in the north, Castella was described by the media as a hamlet, or spot on the map. The locals would most likely describe it as a small piece of bush heaven. It is the perfect change for those of us who came up from the city, yet still close enough to commute when necessary. The people of Castella are a mixed and varied group who usually keep to themselves. You might not speak to them for six months, but there is always a friendly wave when you drive past. Neighbours can be relied on to lend a hand when required.

THIS IS WHERE MY STORY BEGINS, SATURDAY FEBRUARY 7, 2009.

I arrive home at approximately 5:00pm to a sky thick with smoke. The reports on the radio are coming through thick and fast. The one hour drive from the city seemed to take an eternity. I passed flames and smoke near Yarra Glen. It was going to be a long night.

The house I share with my wife and three daughters is perched on the top of a hill. At 435 metres above sea level we are the highest house in our quiet cul de sac. The views to the west are uninterrupted. Kinglake in the distance appears to be overwhelmed by fire. The five kilometres that separate us feels like fifty metres. My stomach tightens. In 2006 we nervously waited for a week as the fire approached. Leaves were caught as they fell out of the sky. This time we would be lucky to start the pumps.

I then run to the shed and gear up; overalls, flannel shirt, boots, cap, mask, gloves, and goggles in my back pocket. I start the pumps. Water surges out of the roof sprinklers. Thank God for that. As I make my way to the house I pass steel bins with water and mops at the ready. My family was well drilled, the fire plan is running smoothly. Gates are opened and animals accounted for. I hook up the fire trailer to the tractor. It gives me little comfort as the sky darkens. Not long after, the power goes out. I kick the

old Honda generator in the guts and off she goes. Generators and electric pumps don't get on well, but cooking the pump is the least of my concerns.

I speak to my neighbour Ralph, who shares our piece of hill, and he tells me his family have already left, but another friend has arrived. Kerry and her young daughter had fled Kinglake, and being unable to escape via the Melba Hwy, they had sought refuge at Ralph's. Kerry tells me that Kinglake is a fireball. The reality of our situation is starting to hit home.

The sky grew darker and darker. It is decided that my girls would bunker down at Ralph's with Kerry and Meg. His house is cut into the hill and the bottom level is double brick. It seems like the best option. At 6.30 p.m. the sky is black. It feels like midnight as I search for a torch.

I would like to think that I have been in a few scrapes and near misses, but even as a policeman for fourteen years I have never been this scared. The situation is out of my control, I just had to hope for the best. The enemy would reveal itself soon enough.

At 6.45 p.m. I continue to stare out towards Kinglake. I hose myself down to keep cool, and then watch as Ralph jumps into the spa fully clothed. Fire makes people do the strangest things. I try not to think what would happen if the wind changed.

Then the phone rings. It is Adrian who lives next door at the bottom of my hill. I casually answer, "How's it going mate?"

He answers, "The fire has just gone past my shed and taken out Ben's ute."

"What are you talking about?" I say.

The urgency in his voice said it all, "It's coming up the hill straight for you!!"

I turn around and am confronted by a wall of flames racing towards my home.

"IT'S COMING UP THE HILL STRAIGHT FOR YOU!!"

Ant sized fire trucks are dwarfed by what is yet to come.

FIGHT OR FLIGHT.

Previous training appears to kick in. In a heartbeat I'm yelling at Ralph and heading for the diesel pump. The pump starts first go. I've got enough adrenalin to start a small car. The sprinklers come alive and I'm running again. I cover the fifty metres to the 10,000 gallon concrete tank in no time and the fire pump sitting on top doesn't let me down. Hose in hand the fight begins.

Everywhere I look there are flames, ten metres high in some places. The sound is like a steam train at full speed, and the heat is intense. I can't breathe without my mask on, and my eyes are burning as I've dropped my goggles.

My heart is thumping and the urge to run is overwhelming. I drop the hose and run to the safer side of the house. The thick mud bricks are reassuring. I find my goggles, take a deep breath and walk back to the hose. Fear slowly converts to anger. The fight in me is back.

The ten metre fire-break I had created, separating us from the bush is helping. The fire is still roaring, but there is very little to burn. The house is wet and the embers extinguish themselves on contact. The wind cuts me a break as it shifts slightly towards the north giving me some breathing space. I'm holding my own.

Time flies and I've been fighting for an hour but it only feels like minutes. I see Ralph out of the corner of my eye. I wonder when he arrived. He's like a man possessed, swinging a wet mop.

The firefront passes and continues north towards Brett's house. Within minutes the gutters are on fire, and flames surround the house. I feel helpless but I pray he's not home.

The spot fires are now out, and the adrenalin switches off. I'm spent. I sit down on the ground and try to comprehend what has just happened. I feel the nightmare is not over yet. I manage to check on the girls, and everyone is safe. My throat is like sandpaper. I down a beer while I watch a section of fence burn. There is no way I could put out the posts, but I need to conserve water for round two.

THE FIRE COMES BACK A SECOND TIME FOR US!
ROUND TWO.

I hear the roar again, before I can see it. Pumps go on again. My wife, Briony, has been coming over regularly to check on me. When she hears the pumps start she rushes over. I try to send her away, but she's here to fight. The fire has come back up the hill, halfway up our driveway.

The southerly wind is howling. Embers fill the sky and fly over the house. The sprinklers are once again doing their job, but there are spot fires starting everywhere, both in front and behind me. I'm struggling to keep up with the hose. The cavalry come to my aid. Briony grabs a mop, while Ralph alternates between the fire trailer and a mop. Grass fires start in the back paddock. We let them burn as they cause no danger.

Two hours go by and the fun is over. I feel like I've gone twelve rounds. The house and sheds are all safe. The pump and fences are easily replaced. Ralph and I share a beer, "Thanks for your help mate." I say.

"I'm sure you'd do the same for me." He replies.

I walk over to Brett's. The house is still standing. Not a scratch on it. I'm soon to find out that fire is a random beast, without explanation.

THE DAY AFTER.

The guys at the start of the street are calling themselves the Castella SES. They missed the main show but are doing a great job of mopping up.

I go and see Adrian and his family. I thank him for the phone call that saved my home. A smile comes to his face as he replies, "No worries mate, want a beer?"

THAT'S CASTELLA!

Photo: HWT

One of Yarra Glens historic railway bridges is engulfed by flames   0.1

YARRA VALLEY ICON DESTROYED IN INFERNO

A shed implodes caught in the firestorm.   0.2

KARDINIA HOMESTEAD BURNS TO THE GROUND

The demise of an original homestead where Prince Charles spent several nights whilst attending Timbertop Boarding School as a youth. This heritage listed building, constructed in the early 1900's, was the original homestead in the area and is surrounded by beautiful vineyards and quality farming properties. Having it burn to the ground on Black Saturday was a great loss to the history of the area.

BEFORE

AFTER

Photo: HWT

0.1 A blanket of thick grey smoke hangs menacingly over the Yarra Valley.
0.2 A spotfire erupts in a Gruyere Vineyard.

GRAHAM HAMILTON

Steels Creek

THE ONLY ROAD OUT WAS
BLOCKED

Graham Hamilton's home was situated on the lower slopes of Steels Creek, a beautiful township in a countryside dotted with wineries. It was also a popular location for trades people who used their acreage properties to run their businesses from home. Graham himself was using his large shed on the property from which he operated his timber joinery business.

Steels Creek, set in the attractive Yarra Valley, was overlooked by a backdrop of the Kinglake hills where any disturbance of the natural peace and tranquility would have been as far away from a person's mind as the bustle of Melbourne's city streets were from Steels Creek.

Saturday the 7th of February 2009 was no exception and the only thing to disturb the quietness was the occasional screech of yellow crested cockatoos as they flew between gum trees….But Graham and other residents had a deep seated fear of a bushfire… perhaps…maybe…

I had been living in Steels Creek for over 35 years, and my knowledge of the bush and the preparations required to reduce fire risk around the property were always my greatest concern. I had kept the grass mown and any dry foliage was always removed to lessen the fire risk. The dam on my property is only approximately 40 metres from my house. Within the neighbourhood we had even established our own fire warning system, which involved an arrangement whereby whoever was the first to see an unusual puff of smoke would broadcast a warning to the others in the area.

THE EXTREME HEAT, THE GUSTY WINDS AND THE DRY SCORCHED LAND

This day the extreme heat, the gusty winds and the dry scorched land had made me feel 'on edge', when late in the afternoon… yes… I could see a huge plume of smoke coming from the north. This looked like a serious fire! The time would have been about 5:30 pm and realizing that I would have a few hours, I started doing some preparations - hosing down the roof, filling the gutters with water and all the rest of the normal fire ready preparations.

At about 6:30pm the phone rang. It was one of my neighbours who lived up on the hill who had a good view of the surrounding area and she said in a frantic voice, "Graham, the fire's coming towards us, what must we do?" I spun around and looked in the direction of the approaching smoke and to my horror and astonishment there was this huge wall of fire coming over the hill towards us. As I was watching this terrifying sight, large embers about a foot long began landing in my garden. I knew at this stage there was no way I could try and defend the house, so I made the decision to evacuate. By now the embers were raining down on us as the firefront approached!

SUDDENLY THESE TREES WERE ENGULFED IN FLAMES

At the bottom of the hill below us is a dense section of mature gum trees. Suddenly these trees burst into flames as the fire swept towards us. This would have been only 500 metres from my house and the roar of the fire was almost deafening… There was panic in the air as the searing winds powered the destructive flames! Everything around us was catching fire as the blaze came at us like a hell bound train!

People from neighbouring properties were hurriedly trying to gather the last of their belongings before they became engulfed in this furious fire. There was only one way out of Steels Creek! It was on a dust road, the width of only one car, and I knew everyone would be using the same road. It is quite a winding road and in one section it is extremely steep. It was escape now or never, so into the car I jumped. Thankfully it started first go and I raced out of the property with the flames licking at the back bumper bar!

I knew that I would probably never see my house again as the inferno was now roaring up behind me. Everywhere you looked, there were violently rotating columns of fire lighting up the surrounds. With heart racing, I went flying down the road as fast as I dared, bumping and crashing over fallen branches, along with the blinding smoke that was making it almost impossible to breathe. As I rounded one corner, there in front of me, at the steep section on the road, was a car with a trailer that had jack-knifed. One of my neighbours had loaded his large tandem trailer with a bobcat and excavator on it, and in the ensuing panic he had forgotten to connect the braking system, resulting in the trailer jack-knifing. Now there was a queue of cars banking up with nowhere to go whilst a black and orange fire filled the sky and the impending inferno bore down on us all.

I KNEW I HAD TO MAKE A SNAP DECISION.

Seeing the resulting strife ahead, I knew I had to make a snap decision. The poor fellow in the car was in such a panic! In my effort to try and calm him down, I told him that trying to save the machinery and the trailer was not

Trees explode and are consumed by the fire leaving no hope for this vineyard.

an option as the fire was now roaring towards us like an express train, and if they didn't move the car and trailer out of the road very soon, we would all be fried alive! The embers were raining down on us and the wind was whipping up a wild dust storm, which combined with the smoke. We hardly knew if it was day or night, it was so thick.

We all pitched in to help, and managed to manoeuvre the machinery off the trailer, somehow. When I think back, I still don't know how we did it. Now with the machinery off, and a bit of damage to the car and trailer, he could pull the car out of the way. The cars all managed to get past and beat a hasty retreat from the inferno that was now crowning over the ridge immediately behind us. My neighbour then managed to get the machines back on the trailer and continue his flee to safety. That little episode in those conditions was like a major catastrophe, and enough to turn anyone insane!

Realising that by now all our houses would be engulfed in fire (most of us carried that thought deep down that maybe 'my house may survive') and with the fire immediately behind us, we raced on down the dust road toward the main Melba Highway. Not knowing which way to go, we turned towards Yarra Glen, which led us to the CFA station in Dixons Creek. Most of us stopped there knowing that would be safer than anywhere else nearby. It was about 7:00pm.

At the station we could hear the CFA's radio going 'non-stop' with calls for help from every quarter. The captain on duty felt absolutely helpless. All his fire trucks were out doing the best they could to save the Steels Creek Township, which had apparently gone up already. I then noticed that once again the glowing embers were falling into the tinder dry paddocks surrounding the fire station and the firefront was racing down the ridge moving rapidly towards us, bursting into the air with great tongues of shooting flames, searching for fuel and oxygen as it started closing in on Dixons Creek. The CFA captain then advised us all to go to Yarra Glen racecourse where there is a large open field with no trees around, which would make it safer for us to stay there. We once again leapt into our cars and gunned it down the highway. Would we make Yarra Glen before the fire jumped the road in front of us, which would have trapped us, leaving us no escape route but to perish in our cars? You think of everything that could go wrong in those moments of extreme pressure. Through much mercy, we got through to the outskirts of Yarra Glen and then made our way to the race course.

PEOPLE WERE CRYING HYSTERICALLY EVERYWHERE!

When we arrived there, we met many of our neighbours, friends and others from the area, but it was terrible… people were crying hysterically everywhere! Some knowing that their loved ones had already been lost in the fire, others not knowing where their fathers, mothers or families were. Never had I witnessed anything as horrifying as the intense grief that these people were stricken with.

The wind had calmed down now (it was approximately 8:00pm), but there was an eerie red glow in the skies all around us. The hills were glowing with burning trees, and it was as if hell had come to earth.

It was there that I met an old friend of mine who used to belong to the CFA. He said we should go back and check on my house. In the back of my mind I thought there just may be a chance that it was still standing. So with the courage of this ex-CFA gentleman and another friend, we headed back towards my house. As we came to each of the police road blocks, they let us through - only because the ex-CFA chap still had his CFA card on him.

We drove down Steels Creek Road… man alive, what a sight met our eyes! We had never seen anything like it… It sure felt like hell as virtually every house we drove past was engulfed in flames. There were cars burning on the side of the road that revealed the efforts of last minute escapes… the debris and trees lying across the road were still burning and more trees were still exploding behind us. The forest was still glowing as a result of the firestorm that had sped through earlier. Whatever next would we see? 'Yes, there is a house still standing…' I still had that feeling – what if???

As we turned off Steels Creek Road and into Hunts Lane (a narrow dust road), nearly every house in the street was burning and it felt as though we were driving through the terrible aftermath of an atomic bomb blast!

We turned the final bend before my house, still in hope, only to see my neighbour's house raging in an absolute inferno. There's no hope I thought… and sure enough there was my property with all the trees around the boundary burning and….Oh no! The hay shed was just a ball of fire! We raced up the driveway, my heart pounding, to find that amazing sight I will never ever forget….

My house was still standing! But wait! Not long and it too would have also gone up in flames. The fire was creeping up slowly burning the short dry grass that was only a couple of feet away from the outdoor deck area! There were small spot fires all around us, which we had to extinguish quickly, otherwise they would be a danger to the house. My two friends and I were frantically running around like headless chooks trying to put out all the spot fires, when all of a sudden a tea-tree bush burst into flames! This was only two feet away from my woodwork shed, which was made wholly from timber, including the exterior cladding – cedar slats. Thankfully I had several large 25 litre buckets on hand and with the dam nearby we had plenty of water, but it also meant plenty of running! Then a large spot fire started under two trees, under which I had a big stack of timber, as well as the trees being extremely dry and flammable themselves! – We just managed to get it out in time, but man, it sure was hard work. We finally managed to save the house and the woodwork shed, but what a day! Without the help of my two friends I could never had done it.

It was now about 2:00am Sunday morning, and it was the first time we could stop to catch our breath since the night before. Mind you, this was not easy either as there was so much smoke still in the air.

I thought I had been prepared and had all my ducks in a row! The first thing I did on Sunday morning was to buy a decent fire pump! But I realise now there was no way anyone could ever have controlled that fire. The terrible dry conditions, the strong winds and the heat… that is what made that day 'BLACK SATURDAY'.

Special thanks goes to Bazza and Whitey. Without them I would never have made it!

IT WAS LIKE HELL...

LONELY FLOWERDALE

FLOWERDALE IS A SMALL TOWN NORTH OF KINGLAKE WEST WHICH LOCALS HAVE DESCRIBED AS THE FORGOTTEN TOWN.

Townsfolk were gathering at the local pub, forty or fifty of them, when a CFA volunteer walked in and advised those who weren't staying to defend, to flee to the safety of Yea, about 30 kilometres to the north. The remaining men then teamed up and made their plan of action. After filling wheelie bins and buckets with water, they saturated the roof and the surrounding ground.

The only CFA truck had been sent off hours earlier to fight another fire, and the sole remaining member of the emergency services – one policeman in his car, decided it was too life threatening to stay and told everyone to leave and flee the fires. He then left himself.

What happened over the next few hours was the devastation of a once attractively decorated township. Two hundred homes were destroyed by the fires and terrible sights were left as the effects of the aftermath were witnessed by those who stayed behind in this tight-knit community.

For three hours these men defended the Flowerdale Hotel, after initially taking refuge in a lineup of fifteen vehicles parked out the front. Spotfires were breaking out all around the property which was miraculously saved by these men armed with hoses, mops and buckets. There was no contact outside the local community as the firefront rolled in on the town. A mother and her two daughters were later found huddled together dead on a road. Another two women were found dead by CFA firefighters, next to their car. A badly burnt man was rescued by his neighbour, only to lose the battle to survive and perish in the back of a ute whilst they tried to escape the ember attack.

DEVASTATED RESIDENTS COMFORT A BADLY BURNT DYING MAN

It was the remnants of a brave and lonely community, void of any fire fighting appliances that finally fled for the refuge of the local pub. The publican and eight others battled for hours to save the pub and local community hall, whilst devastated residents were kept calm inside the hotel, taking shifts to comfort a badly burnt 83 year old dying man.

The fireball that engulfed Flowerdale could be described as a huge blowtorch that mercilessly consumed almost everything in its path. The roads of Flowerdale were still scattered with charred hulks of cars, fallen trees and power lines when officials came through the town checking properties for bodies over the next few days. A red and white ribbon would be tied to the front gate of a property, thus signaling that the property had been checked.

Locals were breaking into tears and shaking with grief as they recalled the experience of finding bodies of children and adults burnt beyond recognition. "We found them and covered them with blankets. We just had to give them a bit of decency," a local resident explained.

0.1 A DOOMED NATIONAL PARK PREPARES FOR THE WORST.

0.2 KILOMETRES OF GRASSLAND AND SCRUB WAS CONSUMED WITHIN MINUTES.

0.3 FIREMEN ON THE ALERT, STRIVING TO PREDICT THE UNPREDICTABLE.

0.4 EXHAUSTED FIREFIGHTERS CATCH A MINUTE OF REPRIEVE BEFORE THE NEXT CALL.

MURRINDINDI, BUXTON
TAGGERTY, FLOWERDALE

FLOWERDALE

Yea

Melba Hwy

Alexandra

Maroondah Hwy

TAGGERTY

MURRINDINDI

MELBOURNE 70KM

Glenburn

Cathedral Range
State park

BUXTON

SEAN O'TOOLE

Murrindindi

SAVED BY THE
RIVER

On February 7th, my three children and I decided to go and camp at Murrindindi Scenic Reserve. It was a very hot day, and it's a great spot to escape the heat. Arriving about lunchtime, we had a quick paddle in the river before some lunch, then erected our tent. For the next hour or so we enjoyed ourselves in, and on the bank of the Murrindindi River.

At around 3:00pm, I noticed a pillar of smoke to the south east of us. The wind was very strong, but going to the north east, away from our position. Moving 25 metres toward the road, it became obvious this was a bushfire. A car then came speeding down the road, and the driver stopped to warn me that the fire had sped up and over the ridge line, and was now only one kilometre down the road. I couldn't believe it was coming our way. How could it move into such a strong wind?

Leaving the tent behind, the kids and I leapt into the car and took off.

As I was about to turn onto the main track, five or six cars in convoy came racing through the smoke and almost collided with me. I slipped into the middle of their line, and drove up the track for about 150 metres, where we were stopped by DSE firefighters. There was a minute or two of confusion with the DSE trying to send us back the way we had come. The group of people I had joined, explained that a fire had already crossed the road and was fast heading towards us. The firefighters told us that the sawmill was on fire as well.

"GET IN THE RIVER!"
We realised we were cut off. The DSE team then told us to "Get in the river!" So we drove into a parking area about fifty metres from the river's edge. **Some of the firefighters cut a path through log barriers and trees, enabling two 4WD's with tanks and pumps, to be driven into the river.** I spent the next ten minutes collecting blankets, drinks, and preparing my very scared kids for what was going to happen. All up, there were about twenty of us. Some of our new friends were beginning to panic, so the firefighters put them into a truck. I put my kids into the second truck and covered the windows with fire blankets.

The guys with the chain saws set about clearing overhanging tree limbs and brush from our immediate area. Others of us dragged this debris a safe distance away. Other firefighters ran hoses from the pumps and started wetting down the surrounding area. A fire tanker joined us, taking care of the spot fires that were starting all around us. We all then began to help, by using Esky lids and small buckets to scoop water onto spot fires. We were completely surrounded, and it seemed as though fire was coming from every direction.

WE CROUCHED BEHIND THE TRUCKS
The main fire came through about an hour after we first entered the river, at about 4:30pm. The smoke was making breathing and seeing difficult. We were being showered by embers which were setting alight everything that wasn't soaking wet. Those with fire blankets sheltered under them, while those of us without, crouched behind the trucks. The heat was intense. Trees around us started burning, but all we could do was make sure we were clear when they fell. Firefighters adjusted the fire nozzles to a wide pattern, to help with the heat and embers, and the guys from the fire tanker, took shelter with us in the river as the fire passed.

By 5:15pm, the firefront had finally passed, and we were able to relax a little. Trees were still burning and falling, but the smoke and heat had cleared. At around 5:30pm, the firefighters started to move us out in small groups, children first. Luckily none of our vehicles were damaged, but the drive out was unreal. One place I intimately knew was totally unrecognisable. Our evacuation point was the old sawmill. An ambulance was waiting, but thankfully, scratches, bruises and sore eyes were the only injuries.

Standing in front of the sawmill where this fire started, we watched as it headed towards Marysville. We didn't know it at the time, but we had just survived the beginning of Black Saturday. If those firefighters hadn't been there, we may not have been so lucky.

THE DSE TEAM TOLD US TO "GET IN THE RIVER"

0.1

0.1 As the firestorm passes overhead, stricken campers take refuge under saturated blankets. **0.2** The only place of safety for these campers is the river as a suspension bridge is surrounded by a ring of fire. **0.2**

A Boeing 737 airliner is dwarfed by the massive smoke plume.

MARYSVILLE
DESTROYED

A SMALL TOWN OF ABOUT 500 PEOPLE WHO GREETED EACH OTHER IN THE STREETS BY NAME, MARYSVILLE HAS NOW CHANGED FOREVER. ONCE A THRIVING TOURIST TOWN, RENOWNED FOR ITS HONEYMOON DESTINATION, IT WAS THE PLACE MELBOURNIANS WOULD ESCAPE TO FOR A WEEKEND OF TEA AND SCONES AT ENGLISH-STYLE GUESTHOUSES.

The relics of the era endure, as does the mood. Marysville is nestled at the foothills of the renowned Lake Mountain snow fields, and was an ideal location to relax and unwind. Once a sawmilling town and the gateway to vast stands of mountain ash, snow gums and beautiful waterfalls, it was an attractive working town responsible for constant supplies of framing timbers for the building industry in Melbourne and surrounds.

0.1 TREES SWAY VIOLENTLY FROM STRONG WINDS WHILE THE SUN IS DIMMED BY THE SMOKE.

0.2 A HUNGRY FIRE DEVOURS ANCIENT FORESTS AND HOMESTEADS

0.3 EXTENSIVE DAMAGE WAS WROUGHT OUT ON THE NARBETHONG SAWMILL.

0.4 A OMINOUS GLOW LOOMS OVER MARYSVILLE.

MARYSVILLE
NARBETHONG

Buxton

Marysville Rd

Maroondah Hwy

MARYSVILLE

Cambarville

NARBETHONG

MELBOURNE 76KM

Reefton

McMahons Creek

Warburton

A BIG BELL IN TOWN THAT RANG A SHUDDER UP YOUR SPINE!

There were once fourteen timber mills, and a big bell in the centre of town that rang a shudder up your spine whenever smoke was seen from nearby watching towers. But up until Saturday 7th February nature had never unleashed its forces on the nostalgic dream town. Even the fires of 1939 had diverted around the township.

Now with no mills, and few jobs for young people, the footy clubs and tennis clubs are gone, and replaced by tourist attractions, holiday houses, snowfield businesses and hire shops. The many accommodation resorts and Bed & Breakfast retreats are the backbone of the town now, along with idyllic eating and dining shops that cater to an older generation of retired or semi-retired customers. They have the time and resources to relax in the leafy township, sheltered by the huge English oaks and deciduous giants that shower the town with autumn colour during fall.

Today was no ordinary day. It was too hot for tourists or anyone else who had been warned in the days leading up to Saturday to keep indoors and away from any fire risk areas.

NARBETHONG'S TUDOR LODGE BURNS!

The fire known as "The Murrindindi complex fire", officially started burning at a disused sawmill at 2:57pm. The flames fanned by wind speeds of up to 120 kilometres per hour pierced through the heavily wooded forests south of Murrindindi, including the aptly named Mt Despair, and reached the township of Narbethong in a finger of fire at about 4:00pm. Narbethong caught alight with many homes under direct flame attack, including the well known Tudor Lodge which was destroyed in the fire.

The wind changed direction soon after, and the wildly burning flank of the fire then became the front of a massive fire that had already wiped out the Narbethong Tudor Lodge and many houses. It now started racing towards Marysville and Buxton with everything in between under severe ember attack.

10 TIMES THE FEROCITY OF A NORMAL BUSHFIRE

The massive flames that had been burning behind Mount Gordon suddenly turn their aggression towards Marysville as the wind change sweeps through.

FLEEING WITH MINUTES TO SPARE!

The Mount Gordon tower DSE fire spotter, Andrew Willans, had warned many people who were in the path of the now horrendous firefront. He fled just before the tower (strategically located on the last hilltop overlooking Marysville) was engulfed in an inferno of hellish flames.

The fire captain in Marysville, Glen Fiske, had been busy all afternoon directing his fire trucks to join strike teams that assisted areas distant from Marysville in fighting the fires. Now just after returning, they prepared for a local onslaught that was to prove too intense, too wild and too ferocious for even 500 tankers, had they been available. All the State's resources could not have saved Marysville that terrible day. It was a supercharged Megafire with ten times the ferocity of a normal bushfire. Convoys of cars fled out of the north end of town towards Alexandra, instructed by several policemen who had driven around the burning township to save as many as they could, evacuating even havens considered safe like the oval and lake area. Belated as it was, it proved a life saving decision for the many who left friends and family who had decided to stay and defend. The fire driven by a roaring wind now cut through the bush abutting the south west perimeter of the town, and spot fires broke out in every nook of the township nestled in a bowl surrounded by gum trees. At 5:45pm the fire siren was heard to sound intermittently in bursts of urgent warning.

By 6:00pm the whole town came under the full venom of a wild firestorm never seen before in its speed and intensity. Glen Fiske had no time to warn his wife Liz and 15 year old son Dalton, who perished in their family home. There was simply no time to evacuate everyone. The fire was so fast that every minute saw kilometres of firefront advance as it overtook vehicles and lives. Even some well prepared fire trained home owners, succumbed to the radiant heat whilst defending their possessions.

CHARRED CHIMNEYS, A BAKERY, A MOTEL AND SCATTERED HOUSES!

The aftermath of a once picturesque town reduced after 146 years of history to burning rubble, left only charred chimneys, a bakery, a motel and scattered houses. This fire came and went before many even knew it had arrived; such was the destroying inferno that engulfed a complete township in its relentless attack on an innocent foe.

The brave, lonely survivors have pictures etched in their minds of the destruction of Black Saturday:- fallen trees uprooted in the wild winds, vivid loss of human lives, and flattened homes of a township of close friends are all remembered from that fatal day. It was terrible to witness the aftermath the next morning, according to the few who lived to tell their story.

MARYSVILLE WILL REBUILD. . .BUT IT WILL NEVER BE THE SAME AGAIN!!!

0.1 WRECKAGE CAUSED BY THE FIRE WAS MORE THAN THE HUMAN MIND COULD COMPREHEND.

0.2 MARYSVILLE PETROL STATION RAVAGED BY FIRE.

0.3 NARBETHONG DEVONSHIRE TEA HOUSE FLATTENED BY THE FIRE'S FORCE.

0.4 NARBETHONG SKI HIRE HAD A SNOWBALL'S CHANCE OF SURVIVAL AS THE WILDFIRE SWEPT THROUGH.

THE FIRE ROARS DOWN MOUNT GORDON, GIVING THE RESIDENTS OF MARYSVILLE ONLY MINUTES TO FLEE.

THE STORY BEHIND THE VIDEO OF MARYSVILLE'S
DESTRUCTION

THE DAY FOR DARYL HULL STARTED LIKE MOST OTHER SATURDAYS.
He worked part time at the 'The Corner Cupboard Cafe' during the day and the 'Crossways Restaurant' during the evening, and Saturday 7th February was the day he had been required to work, so work he did.

The day started hot with little wind movement, but as it wore on the temperature rose sharply and the wind picked up steadily.

There had been fewer visitors than normal, as there had been warnings in the news leading up to the 7th about the extreme weather conditions, and the need for people not to travel around unless they had to. So the day passed a little more quietly than usual.

Daryl went outside after he had finished work for the day. He immediately noticed the tremendous buildup of billowing mountains of smoke in the air out towards Mount Gordon. The winds seemed to pick up from then on changing direction constantly. That's strange, he thought, we haven't heard anything about any fire near here, only a fire near Kilmore! Daryl quickly went to the 'Crossways' and alerted them as to the rapidly building smoke, but since they had not been warned as to any fire nearby, there was little concern; this however very quickly changed. Daryl went back to his cabin and collected his faithful camera. He trained his camera on the smoke and started to video, and what a video!

For the next hour, Daryl videoed the smoke becoming darker and darker, but also there was an incredibly ominous orange glow building up in the smoke. This is not good, he thought. People were still calm in the main, but Daryl thought it was time to head to the oval to think about his path of escape from what he knew in himself must be coming.

Arriving at the oval he was surprised that there was not a person there! The people don't realise what's coming, he thought, but very shortly after this the townsfolk started arriving in cars, looking for a safe haven from the imminent threat. The wind had grown in strength and the smoke was no longer high in the sky, but coming in low through the town. The biggest problem now was the conflicting and confusing stories coming in! Certainly the only way out of town was on the Buxton Road, but it was thought that even Buxton may be on fire! Daryl weighed his options; his boss was pleading with him to join her in a line of cars departing from Marysville, but Daryl had no wish to be caught in a car travelling into unknown territory! Head for the lake he thought, as this had been his thought from years past if they were ever to come under fire threat, with the

little island there he should be safe, and he guessed everybody else would head there as well.

As Daryl videoed the buildup of townsfolk on the oval, a single Police car came screaming in with its lights flashing. A door swung open and a policeman jumped out and started running and shouting "Go, Go, Go!" In a flash people were into cars and going with the Police leading them out. Daryl looked again at the smoke building up and saw for the first time the trees bursting into flame around the oval. This is it he thought, into the lake I go! Daryl had to abandon his cameras at this point, hiding them under a fern at the water's edge. He then swam to the island and lay in the water with it lapping his chin for up to sixty minutes as the fire storm passed over the top of him. The hour Daryl spent in the lake was horrific and startling in the extreme. This ferocious beast came at the town with a fury none could have expected. It wasn't long before everything was going up around him. He sheltered by the island until it too caught fire! At this time the smoke came in low and very thick and dark over his head. It was like midnight and he could feel the fire about to hit with full force. The smoke exploded above him and it rained embers forcing him to sink below the water many times as he swam to the centre of the lake. There was fire everywhere he looked and the noise was extreme, sounding like ten air force jets taking off, but what amazed him was that nobody apart from himself was in the lake! Where was everybody, had they all perished?

A car sped in beside the lake, and another behind it, the first catching fire. Daryl heard voices in panic, but then nothing else!

Daryl finally climbed from the water when he thought it was safe after the main fury had passed. He rested in the mud for a while and then to his relief, he saw flashing blue lights through the dense smoke and realised that someone at least was at the oval. Daryl then made for the oval where he found it full of CFA and DSE vehicles. These poor men had just made an emergency evacuation from Kings Road where they had been trying to stop the fire from sweeping into Marysville, but with the wind change happening at the worst possible moment, they had become trapped and very nearly perished where they fought. Daryl rested for about an hour, drinking water and trying to take stock of things. To Daryl, it felt completely surreal.

Mercifully, Daryl's camera had escaped harm, so bringing it again to his eye he continued to video things that the human eye would never wish to see again.

Trees continued to explode in flames around them for the next few hours, as the wind was still blowing with fury and several times the oval caught fire and had to be brought under control. Daryl filmed all around the oval and realised they were completely surrounded by fire! Houses and buildings, such as the school and the pavilion burnt freely, and Daryl wondered what must be left of the main town. The fire burnt for some time before Daryl could venture from the oval and begin to walk towards the main street, and what destruction that camera recorded! Buildings were still burning fiercely and as Daryl walked, he realised that if anything was left of Marysville, it wouldn't be much! Daryl went as far as he dared up the main street, always on the lookout for the red hot flying embers and the fiercely venting gas bottles. Finally he decided he had seen enough for a life time, let alone that one night. The 'Cross Ways' was still standing, so Daryl helped for the next four hours or so putting out spot fires. He then rested there for a few hours as by then it was 4:00am on Sunday morning. Finally daylight dawned over the ridge, and the destruction that met his eyes could never be described! He took his faithful camera again and traversed the main street. It was enough to break a man's heart and indeed it broke and destroyed many people's lives! Trees were down everywhere, buildings were still smoldering and burning freely, cars had collided with trees and in one case a water main had burst, covering the car in a fountain of water. Brick walls had toppled and broken like children's toys, buildings had crumbled; death was everywhere.

Daryl turned away and headed for the oval once again, stopping at the lake to view the place where his life had been spared. Continuing on to the oval, he saw a helicopter buzzing overhead and he realised that the first human life from outside the town had arrived!

Finally others made their way in to Marysville and Daryl was able to get out by driving to Alexandra, before he was to return to his home in Melbourne. There he pondered and relived that fateful day when the fire storm consumed Marysville, destroying a way of life, a country charm and a community that will struggle to refit the jigsaw pieces that used to link so closely together.

0.1

0.1 Only the stark shell of the famous 'In Neutral' store remains as its contents burn.
0.2 Fire ravages a main street of Marysville.

0.2

0.3 Unique homesteads are reduced to ashes.
0.4 Marysville's attractions are consumed by the inferno.

0.3

0.4

DAVID NICHOLLS

Narbethong

SAVED FROM THE
JAWS OF DEATH

We knew it was to be a terrible day, so I went down that morning to Narbethong CFA Station where I was based as a volunteer, to make sure the fire truck was fuelled up, full of water and ready for action ... just in case!

I checked my yellow CFA suit and found that helmet, boots and gear were all in place. Satisfied everything was fine, I went back home. Never in my wildest dreams did I realise what lay ahead later that day.

We had just one truck based at Narbethong and the nearest CFA Station was at Marysville, which was about ten kilometres away, with Mount Gordon in between. The radio tower for CFA communications was on top of Mount Gordon which overlooked Marysville to the east. Marysville has three trucks based there normally, but today was not a normal day. Due to the high fire risk, two strike teams were sent there in the afternoon, each consisting of five trucks and four men per truck. The main purpose of a strike team is to catch a fire early before it has time to break out, and control the fire with a containment line.

Looking back, I am certain that no amount of preparation or quantity of fire trucks, could ever have been sufficient to meet the intensity and speed of the fire that day. The high winds, raging temperatures, and vast areas of tinder dry fuel that the drought had caused, was a recipe for disaster, and the best planned operations were to prove incapable of saving the great number of houses and the precious lives we were trained to protect.

I headed home that morning, and enjoyed playing with our little boy, Lachlan, who was 4 years old. The wind was strong and hot, so I spent most of the time inside. One of my mates from Narbethong came to the house that morning, and we had a couple of hours talking together. At about 3:30pm, I noticed some smoke towards the north, which was in the Murrindindi area. I guess it was about thirty kilometres away, and even though the wind was fierce, the distance provided some sense of security. Subconsciously, my CFA training was at work. Uncertain as to what lay in store, after talking it over with my wife, Nicole, I decided to go back to the station to pick up my gear in case the need arose. I drove back to Narbethong, only a ten minute run, and grabbed my CFA suit, helmet and gear and came back to the house.

FIFTEEN MINUTES AFTER MY WIFE DROVE OUT, THE FIRE ARRIVED!

By this stage, the billowing smoke clouds were only about a kilometre away, and it prompted me to get Nicole to take the car and go to her parents house in Healesville, with our darling little Lachlan. We weren't overly concerned at the smoke, as the area had been covered in smoke before, but as a precaution we decided to play it safe. As she drove out of the driveway, I put my CFA fireproof suit on and prepared for whatever lay ahead. Only fifteen minutes after my wife drove out of the gate, the fire arrived. I had thought the worst of the smoke was just about over, but realised later it had only just begun.

A large cleared farm paddock to the north of our house was our only safety barrier between us and the National Park. A row of gum trees followed the fence line of our property and the neighbouring houses in our street. Suddenly, the grass paddock started breaking out in spot fires, as embers from the forest fire were thrown forward in an advancing onslaught. I had started the fire pump, and was saturating the house and bushes around it, but in no time the trees lining our property at the end of the no through road were alight. The roar of the fire was deafening. The timber house of our neighbour then caught alight, as

I KNEW I COULDN'T DO MUCH TO SAVE OUR HOUSE

A charred ute among the remains of David Nicholls' property.

nearby trees raged with fire, and the flames from their house were blowing against the wall of our cedar house some twenty metres away. I knew I couldn't do much to save our house, without putting out the neighbour's fire. That being impossible, I trained the water on to the side of our house but everything was going up around the house – grass, trees, bushes and then the house caught alight.

I looked in horror at my neighbour's house, totally ablaze, and I could see the house next to theirs also burning – a brick home that had caught fire in the roof, before the flames surged through the ceiling and overtook the remainder of the house in minutes. Both the neighbours had fought with courage, but had left only minutes earlier, before I also scrambled out with my life.

With our house now burning fiercely, I raced inside and grabbed our precious box of photos. On the top, lay the leather album of our wedding photos.

WITH THE BACK OF THE UTE ABLAZE I SET OFF DOWN THE DUST ROAD!

In the minutes that followed, the main firefront arrived with explosions and the noise of a jet plane seemingly just over my head. I ran to the ute, a Ford F100, and put the box of photos on the passenger seat. Several other household items had been hastily thrown in the back of the ute only minutes before, and these were now burning with ember attack from the fire. I jumped into the driver's seat – this was now my only hope of escape, as my wife had taken the car, and with the back of the ute ablaze, I tore off down the dust road. Explosions were going off all around me as I neared the end of the street, where it intersected with the main road to Narbethong.

I stopped briefly at the corner house, where an elderly lady, hysterical with the fire, had stayed behind, possibly afraid to leave the safety of her house. She managed to get to the passenger door of the ute, where I yelled at her over the thundering noise of the fire to come around to the driver's side. Due to the photo box taking up the left hand seat, I jumped out and held the door open for her to climb into the centre, but she didn't appear. Frantically, I yelled to her through the thick smoke, but there was no reply. I waited another 10 - 15 seconds hoping she would appear, so I could get her into the centre seat, but after yelling out many times amidst the roar of the firestorm, it was to no avail – she never appeared. The smoke was so thick I couldn't see the front of the bonnet from the cab.

THE FIRE OVERTOOK ME AT 150 KILOMETRES PER HOUR

In desperation, with the back of the ute now raging with fire, I drove frantically, with my heart thumping in my chest, at speeds of up to 120 kilometres per hour towards Narbethong. The firefront thrust forwards ahead of my burning vehicle and overtook me. I reckon that the fire was travelling at 150 kilometres per hour. A minute or two later, there was a loud explosion, and the rear window of my ute, ravaged by fire and heat, blew out of the back in an ear-splitting bang. I was now in unprotected attack from the full force of the fire and radiant heat. Seconds later, a huge gum tree fell across the road immediately in front of me, and I slammed through the bushy section of the upper part of the tree. With one wheel torn from the front axle, I careered another 90 metres down the bitumen road until the ute came to a grinding halt – never to go again.

I threw myself into a ditch! Grabbing our leather wedding album, I leapt from the burning vehicle and ran as fast as I could, expecting the LP gas tank of the vehicle to explode at any moment. In my frantic dash, I searched the roadside to find a spot that wasn't burning, for any hope of survival. With the smoke of the burning eucalypt trees all around tearing at my lungs, I threw myself into

a ditch that was void of grass and other burning debris. I thought again of the elderly lady – I knew she couldn't have survived in my ute anyway, and I was just hoping she had got to safety somehow. (I found out later, she perished in the fire as she tried to escape.)

Pulling my CFA collars up around my neck, and with the protective helmet covering my head and neck, I buried my head into the leather photo album. Not knowing whether I would live to see my wife again, I huddled into the ground, gasping each breath from the oxygen-depleted air that was swirling wildly around me. It seemed like an eternity that I lay at the roadside, while the fire thundered over me like a steam engine on fire. I did not dare once lift my head, as each time I attempted to, the searing heat lunged at my face like a thousand needles piercing my skin.

About 20 minutes later, above the noise of the fire, I heard what I thought was the motor of a vehicle. I lifted my head to see a ute making its way along the debris-littered road. I jumped up and waved my arms for it to stop. What a feeling of relief I felt as one of my CFA colleagues yelled to me to jump in! I stumbled to his ute through the heat and collapsed into the back of it. I can still remember the feeling of being plucked from the burning, as we weaved along the road, picking our way through the fallen burning branches to the blazing township of Narbethong.

WATER WAS POURED OVER MY DEHYDRATED BODY!

As we neared the CFA station, our attention was caught by a pair of waving arms beckoning us into the carpark of the Ski Hire store across the road from the CFA Station. The Mystic Mountain store, with its large basement, was like a beacon on a stormy night. It was a refuge for more than thirty people who sheltered there that fire-ravaged afternoon. I was totally spent and in desperate need of water, as I collapsed in the safety of the basement under the shop. Water was poured over my dehydrated body. The heat of the last hour had taken its toll. I couldn't stand up, and my overheated body gradually returned to a more reasonable temperature level, while I drank slowly and steadily to replace the fluid I had lost from sweat and exhaustion, and the debilitating inferno that had sapped my body.

My next concern was to help others during the fire attack, as we were taught. My CFA training was lying idle, while I was not holding a hose in these precarious conditions.

Due to the fallen trees all over the road, the fire truck had not yet left Narbethong, but it had been used to hose spot fires that lit up the surrounding trees around the shop. The use of the fire pump had unfortunately run the battery flat. We were able to tow start the fire truck with the help of a vehicle owned by a tourist who had sheltered in the basement with us. Once up and going, I fought the fires with our crew of four putting out burning houses, sheds, and fences, even using the path through the fallen gum tree I had cleared with the ute, that now lay a burnt out wreck a little nearer to town. A strike team from Marysville had tried to assist us with our plight during the initial onslaught, but had turned back under fire attack, and retreated to the Marysville Oval. It would have been certain peril if they had tried to get through to Narbethong. As it was, they had to drive back past burning houses, in an effort to get the fire truck to a place of relative safety from the hell that was breaking out all around Marysville.

By 4:00am, totally exhausted, we were forced to stop for the night and get some rest. What a day of days! After a reassuring phone call to my wife to set my mind at rest, I took a well-earned sleep.

Valuable equipment in a machine shop becomes a warped mound of scrap metal.

IAN & JACQUI PEARSON

Marysville

HOUSES ERUPTED IN FLAMES
ALL AROUND US!

THE FIRE AT MURRINDINDI'S DISUSED SAW MILL SITE IGNITED ON SATURDAY AFTERNOON FROM UNKNOWN CAUSES.

Jacqui noticed smoke in the sky soon after that, prompting me to look up the CFA and DSE websites on the internet. The sites confirmed the location of the fire and this later became known as the Murrindindi complex fire.

No size was mentioned, and despite checking the website regularly for any updates, I didn't get any further details. By 4:30pm the Murrindindi blaze had thrust through the forest like a piercing finger and Narbethong was under full fire attack. We had been on a high alert for the past three days and the state was warned so many times that Saturday was going to be the worst conditions in living history for bushfires in Victoria. I cannot understand how anyone could say we weren't warned. We were warned time and time again. It was going to be 47° Celsius, the state was dry as all heck and the wind was going to be ferocious.

My wife had taken the warnings more seriously than I and had pre-packed some essential items for her 87 year old mother who lives in her own separate house on the property. Our two acre property consists of the main house, Jacqui's mother's house and two B&B suites.

Talking through our fire plans, we decided that if there was a fire threat, we would evacuate Mum and our dog to a safe retreat so that Jacqui and I could concentrate on defending the house. Our fire plan training at CFA community meetings in the town had given us the confidence to stay and defend and we resolutely began putting our fire plan into action over the next hour or two.

THE HOT NORTH WIND PUSHING AGAINST US

The sky was now a deep orange glow and with the hot north wind pushing against us, Jacqui took several photos of the looming inferno bearing down on us.

Delderfield Cottages — miraculously saved!

We had accumulated about six wheelie bins over the years. Rounding up the 300 litre bins we stationed them at points all around the house and filled them with water. I got up on the roof between about 4:30 to 5:00pm and plugged the down pipes on two sides of the house and filled the gutters with water. The sky was blackening with smoke and it was becoming obvious we were going to be coming under fire attack.

With some premonition of the danger, preparing for the worst, Jacqui had collected all our family photos and important documents together. Never before had Marysville been hit by fire. Even in 1939 when a lot of the state was ablaze, the fire only reached the edge of the town and was stopped. What lay ahead was to be a drastic change to the whole of Marysville's landscape, possibly never to be the same again.

We had cleared an area on the north side of the house, but this fire was to break all rules and it actually came from the south west.

At about 4:40pm there was a wind change. This caused the pathway of fire that had pierced through the forest from Murrindindi, which was attacking Narbethong township, to shift towards the East. This narrow pathway of fire now became a massive firefront and was rapidly approaching Marysville and Buxton.

FORGET THE WINE, YOU'RE GETTING OUT NOW!

Marysville is situated in a bowl with mountains on all sides. The fire actually ended up surrounding three sides of the town causing incredible difficulties. At about 5:00pm Jacqui went into mum's house and told her it was time to come into the main house. Jacqui's mum exclaimed, "I've just poured myself a glass of wine so….."

Jacqui replied, "Forget the wine, you're getting out now!" Mum had no idea of the seriousness of the situation, but she obliged with Jacqui's voice of urgency.

Mum responded, "I can tell in your voice you are really serious about this and I think I've been told to shut up."

Jacqui said, "Don't ask any questions Mum, because I don't know the answers."

Around 6:00pm Jacqui had her mum in the car and decided to take her down to the Cumberland convention centre (which later burnt to the ground). When she got there, Jacqui was told that everyone was evacuating, so she should keep going. Jacqui joined a convoy and started heading out of the town. All she was worried about was watching the bumper bar of the car in front, not knowing whether they were heading into another fire. She could only see about four metres ahead of them. Buxton was still OK and an official was waving everyone on as fast as he could. "Keep going! Go! Go! Go!"

I CRAWLED OUT FROM BENEATH A MASSIVE GUM TREE THAT HAD FALLEN RIGHT ON TOP OF ME!

When Jacqui left Marysville, I changed into my heavy jeans, a big thick jumper and put my hat and goggles on. I got my mop and bucket and started patrolling the house waiting for the fire. Soon after, the wind really picked up and started roaring through the trees. It was as loud as a jumbo jet just above my head. The house diagonally across the road erupted into flames and within ten minutes it was just a pile of burning rubble. It was unbelievable, but this was just the beginning. I was checking the outside of the house and was walking down the gravel drive with a torch in one hand (it was getting dark) and a mop in the other. Suddenly, with the wind howling in my ears, I was planted face down into the gravel. I crawled out from beneath a massive gum tree that had fallen right on top of me across the driveway. The roar of the wind had prevented me from even hearing it fall. It was a seriously big tree with an enormous butt. With my mop broken in half and my hand bleeding badly, I checked that no bones were broken, and kept up my duty with a new mop I grabbed from the house. The tree had crashed onto the carport in front of the B&B suite, and I realised later how close I had come to death. My broken mop was less than a metre away from the main trunk of the tree. It was so close. This was incredible. I had no thought of leaving because we had previously made the decision to stay and my adrenalin was by now flowing at a million miles an hour.

With the fire starting to engulf houses all around us now, I was full time putting out spot fires with buckets of water from the wheelie bins. The mains water went off; I had no water at all due to the burst mains in other parts of the village. It was just the wheelie bins and a bath full of water that I would rely on for the next few hours of fire fighting.

I COULDN'T SEE MY HAND IN FRONT OF ME

The police had starting evacuating many houses by now and had warned most people to get out. Buildings all around us were aglow except for a few houses that were still OK. With almost nil visibility and the wind screaming, I couldn't see my hand even if I held it right in front of my face, it was so black. The noise was unbelievable and I realised the full force of the firefront was hitting town behind the first ember attack 30 minutes earlier. I came indoors for about 40 minutes whilst the main front of the fire was ripping through the town. I remember looking out the front window and seeing a roll of burning gas crossing the nature strip. The grass was short and green, so there was nothing to burn, but this just looked like a steamroller of burning gas charging towards the property. It was blazing like hell out there. I had to put wet towels behind every external door and felt confident

the fire plan was working well. It was exactly what we had planned to do. I climbed up into the roof space several times during the night to check that there were no embers blowing in. On one occasion I noticed some fine glowing embers were getting through the roof ventilators, but these were floating down on to the fibreglass insulation batts and self extinguishing, so they seemed OK to leave. As soon as the firefront had passed, I went outside while the heavy embers were still attacking the house. One of the stumps on the corner of the house was burning badly, with several baseboards burnt right through at the corners. I quickly worked at putting these out with buckets of water and continued my vigil with the mop and bucket. Jacqui rang me in the middle of it all to let me know she had got out, but she was stopped at the police roadblock on the way back and was told she couldn't come back to Marysville to help me. Later in the evening, at about 9:00pm, I spoke to Jacqui again to let her know that the house had been saved, but the fire was still going in the woodpile.

By this stage my water supply had run right out except for a few buckets I had kept for inside emergencies. Everything around me had an orange glow to it. Spot fires kept breaking out round the house during the evening. The woodpile right next to our garage then caught alight; it may have been smouldering for some time, but seeing as I had no water, I was helpless and a short time later the garage burnt to the ground.

AT ABOUT 2:00AM THE NEIGHBOUR'S HOUSE CAUGHT ALIGHT!

Whilst it was still burning fiercely a fire truck drove in. It was obviously too far gone, but the firemen gave me real encouragement and they were ready to do anything to help. One of the firemen had just lost his wife and son in their own house fire and the house next door they had come to put out happened to be the same fireman's brother's house. They hosed down the gable of our house, as it was getting pretty hot by then, but they were helpless to save our neighbour's house.

Then the house two along, which had still been OK until then, suddenly caught alight. Racing out of our property, the firemen went to try and save it, but in minutes it was also gone and every effort to put it out failed. It would have been about 6:00am Sunday before I finally shut my eyes for a sleep. I couldn't get through to Jacqui as all phone contact was lost. Two days later I finally got through to her to let her know I was all right. It had been an agonizing wait for her.

LOOKING BACK NOW, I THINK HOW CLOSE I CAME TO LOSING MY OWN LIFE AND I THINK WHY, WHY, WHY???

Photo: Newspix

Marysville flattened.

THE THRIVING 'IN NEUTRAL' RESTAURANT

DESTROYED!

THE PICTURESQUE STEAVENSON FALLS

RAVAGED!

MARYSVILLE'S FAMED MAIN STREET SHOPS

WRECKED!

MARYSVILLE LAKE AND BEYOND

SCORCHED!

A TRANQUIL FOOT BRIDGE

CHARRED!

A QUAINT COUNTRY CHURCH

CONSUMED!

PETER RICE
Alexandra

ACTION STATIONS

THE STORY OF BLACK SATURDAY STARTED A LOT EARLIER THAN SATURDAY 7TH OF FEBRUARY 2009.

On the Tuesday and Wednesday prior, we had been sending out warnings to the other emergency departments such as the Police, council, the media and mainly the local radio station.

With the weather man saying we would be having winds of up to 100 kilometres per hour and temperatures up to 46°C, we knew with that weather pattern, coupled with the already severe twelve year drought, we would have real trouble and needed to warn people.

The CFA Incident Control Centre here in Alexandra includes over twelve brigades in total, so I made sure all the captains from each station had been fully briefed as to what this day could bring forth!

On Saturday, I arrived at the station at about 7:30am. We did a full radio test to make sure all the stations' radios were in working order and I then checked the weather forecast estimates again. There was no change to the existing conditions and every preparation possible was finalized. The weather forecast had remained unchanged! We finished setting up the multipurpose room at the joint Emergency Services Facility as an Incident Control Centre (ICC) and tested all communications and the layout should it be needed. Between 12 to 15 staff commenced duties progressively during the Saturday morning.

The weather started hot, but with no wind, and by 10:00am people were starting to say the weather people had got it wrong! I was watching the wind meters in the upper hills and could see they were gathering strength. I knew it wouldn't be long before we also felt the wind!

At 10:57am I went outside and felt the first breath of north-west wind against my face. Here we go I thought! It was 38°C by now and I knew the temperature would rise fast with the wind behind it.

Nothing much was happening in the Centre, so I took a break for an early lunch. After lunch we got the first report of a fire at Kilmore, it was now 12:20pm. I sent out a pager message to all brigades telling them the weather was turning nasty and to man the stations now!

I soon realised, while listening to the CFA radio traffic that things weren't going well at Kilmore and at 1:28pm I had the first request for our staging trailer. Two minutes later I had a request for our media liaison officer, then at 1:47pm I received the first request for a strike team! Action stations! I paged the

pre-organized strike team and told them to meet as a convoy at Molesworth. They met there at 2:30pm and started heading to Kilmore urgently!

A FIRE HAD STARTED AT MURRINDINDI!

At 2:57pm I had my first call from CFA Yea Group Headquarters saying that a fire had started at Murrindindi. I quickly realised that we would need the strike team back that was heading to Kilmore, so I urgently sought permission to divert, as by this time they were outside my area of control. Communications congestion delayed this for about twelve minutes, which was terribly frustrating. Once arranged, they were told to attend the Murrindindi mill area urgently!

The Yea CFA Group Officer, Neil Beer, rang again and said they had serious trouble and could I dispatch another strike team in addition to the first one? I quickly paged the second team and ordered their immediate departure.

I went outside again and looked towards the Black Range which is behind the station. Judging by the immense column of smoke, I knew the fire was big and growing fast. Rushing inside, the decision was made to retrieve our resources from Murrindindi, which was implemented. These two strike teams, plus the few remaining tankers I had left, were then redirected to deploy to the Narbethong area as I could foresee that being threatened later.

Chaos was building in the Control Centre as we had just lost power. Thankfully the generator had kicked in, but this only ran our emergency control systems and not the air conditioning! We soon had sweat dripping down our faces as it was now about 42°C outside! I arranged for the local radio station, UGFM, to re-emphasize earlier warnings for people in the Narbethong and Buxton areas and beyond, as there was a major fire developing out of control on the Black Range, spreading south-east from Murrindindi. My concern at the emerging situation was passed up the chain as well as to the local DSE and Police.

THE FIRE HAD ALREADY CROSSED THE HIGHWAY!

The two strike teams arrived at Buxton and told me they could go no further as the fire had already crossed the highway! This surprised me, but what surprised me more was that just a little earlier I had been watching the head of the fire from the back of the station, and when I walked back inside, there were messages coming in on the two-way radio that houses in Narbethong were on fire! "This can't be correct," was my first exclamation! Then the pagers started going off with the same reports.

I did a quick calculation and realised that the main fire was spotting up to twenty kilometres ahead of the main fire! Reports were coming in that embers 400mm long were being blown into town and starting fresh fires. Never before in my 40 years of firefighting have I heard or seen embers travel so far in front of the main front!

The wind was like a tornado outside and the temperature was touching 47.2°C. I checked the humidity and saw it said 7%, with wind speed 80 kilometres per hour here and up to 120 kilometres per hour at firefront!

THE PAGERS WERE GOING BALLISTIC!

The pagers were going ballistic! I realised things were going bad, very fast!

I contacted both strike teams and instructed them to go directly to Marysville, as I realised that they also would be coming under ember attack very soon.

The two strike teams arrived in Marysville at 6:24pm and joined up with the one tanker already there. The DSE were also there with three or four trucks. Spot fires were already starting in the Kings Road area, so it was decided to send the trucks into this area urgently! At 6:40pm I put out a Red flag alert to all the firemen telling them the wind change was imminent! A few minutes before 7:00pm the wind changed like a cyclone! The wind change could not have come at a worse time. With the fire now travelling along the edge of Marysville, the wind change meant the whole side of the fire became a new major and uncontrollable front. The strike teams were urged to get out of

Kings Road and down to the oval. All trucks left immediately, apart from two tankers from Yarck. One was stuck completely, and the men had to leave it and climb onto the other one. Finally they made it to the oval, but not before extensive damage and injured firemen!

I was in constant contact with the strike teams and knew things were going very badly. I was frantically sending as many tankers as I could to Marysville, but by now I had very few trucks left. The trucks I did send couldn't get in anyway, so they started working to save Buxton and Taggerty!

"MARYSVILLE GONE!"

The leader of one of the strike teams contacted me and said the two words I will never forget for the rest of my life, "MARYSVILLE GONE!"

I was frantic, sweat was pouring down my face, and visibility was down to about one to two metres in the Control Centre because of the thick smoke pouring in! I was trying to make contact with the Narbethong tanker, but had been unable to reach it by radio. I tried for several hours to get through, but to no avail! I finally rang my counterpart at Lilydale, Group Officer Ken Reid and asked if they could send a truck from their end over the Black Spur, but the reply was, "We have no trucks ourselves!" They offered to send a command car, to which I agreed! Somehow this car made it over the Spur and into Narbethong to find the tanker, but little else! The firemen had been too busy to check their radio.

A picturesque town – Annihilated!

During this whole ordeal, the pagers had been continually going off. Calls came from people trapped in houses, trapped in cars, down dirt roads, on foot, just about everywhere. We received close to 1000 pager calls that day and to over 80% we had to say there was no hope, and we couldn't do anything to help! In total we took 11,000 phone calls over the four weeks the fires were burning.

The townsfolk were also coming to the station, as panic was building up in Alexandra. The pressure was intense! I had trucks deployed and needed more. After frequent attempts, due to congestion, I finally made contact with the CFA Regional Emergency Coordination Centre at Seymour and pleaded for strike teams. To my relief, I was told that strike teams were on their way from Seymour, Wangaratta, Mansfield and even across the border in NSW!

THE MEN STOOD SHOULDER TO SHOULDER AND FINALLY HELD THE FIRE!

They started to arrive later that night and we stationed them at Taggerty, where we had decided to put everything into stopping the fire hitting the town. The wind had dropped a bit and the temperature had cooled somewhat. The men stood shoulder to shoulder and finally held the fire not more than 100 metres from the town! They were still fighting well into Sunday morning.

The DSE and CFA combined were working a major Level 3 Incident Control Centre from around 4:00pm on the Saturday, with the DSE as the Controlling Agency. I became the Deputy Controller from the Sunday morning shift.

Finally things calmed down and at 4:00am on Sunday morning I drove home to try and catch some sleep. I had to be back at command by 7:00am and I found sleep wasn't going to come easily. With three or four towns that had been wiped out in your command centre area, sleep is the furthest thing from your mind!

The crews and all management staff did an absolutely sterling task under unprecedented and horrific conditions. All of them deserve medals. Whilst there were terrible losses, all can be proud that many hundreds of buildings were saved, loss of life was minimized to the least extent possible and that many towns that could have been destroyed remained intact. Nothing more could have been done at a local level. Whilst most losses were on Black Saturday, the Murrindindi fire operation remained one of the biggest ever in Australia, lasting for over a month in remote bush locations before the fire was finally brought under control.

JOHN DRYSDALE

Yarck

SAVED BY A FOG NOZZLE!

During the week leading up to Saturday 7th February, we had been warned again and again that an extreme day was looming. We had heard such warnings many times before, but these days had not always eventuated. But this time it seemed different because the weeks leading up to it had been extremely and unusually hot. The day arrived and I did a few chores around our farm before heading to the Yarck fire station at about 11:00am. By now the wind was picking up and quite a few of the other CFA members were arriving. After waiting around for a while, we heard about the Wandong fire which had just started. This wasn't good news.

Our captain, Tom Jones, and I, as first lieutenant, worked out crews for the tankers available there at the time. Marty Shaw, our second lieutenant, had already been asked by the Alexandra group to be a strike team leader, so he headed to Alexandra with another member as his penciller/record keeper. Our strike team was called for and we were to meet at Molesworth at 2:30pm. Our second tanker truck was also requested and after some discussion we sent it with Dick Sinclair, our fourth lieutenant, as crew leader and two other crew members. The heat and wind became worse as we waited. At 3:00pm we heard that a fire had started at Murrindindi, so we prepared a team with four other members on the tanker and myself as crew leader. At 3:30pm we received a phone call urgently requesting our strike team to move immediately to the Murrindindi Mill. We were numbered strike team 1250.

As we travelled toward Murrindindi we heard radio messages from Marty Shaw's strike team 1204, enquiring whether they should return to Murrindindi as they were only at Trawool. They were told to continue at this stage but within a few minutes were asked to return; such was the uncertainty of where crews were most needed on the day with new fires starting all over the place all the time.

We arrived at Murrindindi at approximately 4:00pm, just before strike team 1204. We heard on the radio that a vehicle had just arrived out of the bush, but that four other cars that had been following it, hadn't made it out. I instantly thought, "This really doesn't sound good!"

We put out fires on the edge of the river and near the bush and then did some asset protection at the Mill offices. By now we needed to refill our water tanks so we headed to a nearby creek. On the way there we heard that Narbethong was under severe ember attack. The OK came to leave Murrindindi and we were to rendezvous at Buxton for orders. The time was now about 5:00pm. On our way to Buxton, it was encouraging to hear news that some DSE guys had returned out of the bush with the four missing carloads. Seventeen people, including children, were all now safe and well, apart from some smoke inhalation. The very courageous DSE people, who went in to save these residents and bring them out to safety, did so at the risk of their own lives. When lives are at risk people go to amazing lengths to save them.

FAMILY TAKES REFUGE IN A TIMBER KILN WITH FIRE ALL OVER IT

On arrival at Buxton we were told to get to Kings Road, on the southern fringe of Marysville, as soon as possible to start back burning, in the hope of saving Marysville township. We acted on these orders immediately. As we left Buxton and headed to Marysville, a resident stopped us on the road and pleaded with us to radio through a message asking to get a helitanker to make a water drop on a hardwood drying kiln at a nearby timber mill. His mate had called him and told him that he and his family, five of them, were inside the kiln and there was fire all around them. I urgently made a call to our strike leader and told him about this grim situation, but I doubted whether aircraft could fly by this time because of the incredibly intense smoke and high winds. I didn't hold out much hope. Things were getting really desperate.

(Much later, on giving my statement to the police I found out that fifteen people got out of that kiln alive, so I felt heaps better, even if it had nothing to do with our call!)

On the way from Buxton to Marysville the thick smoke on our right looked horrific. We took note of some green paddocks on the edge of the road for safe refuge areas if the need arose. I told the crew to ensure all personal protective equipment was on – helmet, goggles and gloves. "Look out for each other, as this doesn't look good," I instructed... "and good luck!"

FIRE AND FLAME ... AS HIGH AS YOU COULD SEE

We arrived at Kings Rd at 6:00pm having heard on the radio along the way that a wind change was due in about an hour. The change would be to a strong south-westerly. The DSE guys, who had been waiting for us to arrive, started back burning between the edge of Kings Rd and a spot fire that had already started. We had nine tankers between our strike teams, plus the number two Marysville tanker as well and also about ten DSE slip-ons (fire fighting four wheel drive vehicles). We lined the edge of Kings Rd for asset protection - to stop falling embers from igniting the houses. We had hooked on to a hydrant, but there was very little water due to too many users and the power going out. The burn was going well – very hot but heading away nicely driven by a strong wind. However, literally within minutes, the wind direction changed radically as the fresh south-westerly powered through. We were working on spot fires around houses one minute and the next moment there was fire and flame from the ground to as high as the eye could see!

Strike Team Leader Captain Tom gave us the call to get out, as it had already gone over us and was burning behind the houses. We started to pack up the hoses and I told the crew to "Get in and we're out of here!" As we finished packing up the hoses, I noticed the tanker 2 crew in extreme trouble on the opposite side of the road. The fire was pouring over and under their truck and they couldn't get in it. I immediately instructed some of my crew to give me the hose and turn it back on, as I rushed to their assistance.

I DIDN'T HOLD OUT MUCH HOPE. THINGS WERE GETTING DESPERATE.

0.1 Scattered sheet iron and gas bottles shows the force that was encountered.

0.2 Branches ripped down by the high winds lay strewn across the roads creating mayhem for those fleeing the area.

0.1

0.2

THE FOUR OF US GOT UNDER THE FOG NOZZLE

I doused it down as best I could to try and quell the flames, but the heat and wind were just too much for us. I made the call to "GET OUT" as the heat and flames were forcing us back. I got to the back of our truck and crew leader Dick, from tanker 2, called his men to come around the front of our truck. Dick fought through the heat, sustaining minor burns in the intense flames. The other crew members turned our water hose onto a fog nozzle setting (a fine misty spray of water from the fire hose which creates a 'fog of water' for protection). The four of us got under the fog nozzle for air and moisture, as the hot air was scorching our airways. The wind was driving the heat at us so hard that we were pinned where we were and couldn't move to get in the truck for about five minutes. Finally there was a lull in the wild wind and we made a dash for the cab. There were four of us and, out of the smoke, we suddenly met two other crew members from tanker 2. These guys were also desperate for relief because, unbeknown to us, they had still been trapped behind their tanker.

"KEEP GOING STEADY AND WE MIGHT MAKE IT."

Thankfully we were all able to scramble in and move off only to find two trees had fallen over Kings Road blocking our escape - one had fallen from each direction as the wind was choppy. It was decided to drive towards the fire and try to get around the first tree and then towards the house side to get around the second one. With visibility at about five metres, at one stage we drove into a gutter and then a tree cracked into the windscreen. I said to our driver, "Keep going steady and we might make it. Go too fast and we won't!" Thankfully, Dan was a very experienced driver and did a fantastic job.

Turning the clock back a bit, while we were assisting the tanker 2 crew, all the other tankers and DSE personnel had evacuated to Gallipoli Park and Captain Tom had been terribly concerned that he hadn't been able to contact either of the two Yarck tankers. I guess he thought he'd lost us.

We continued slowly down Kings Rd in pitch darkness, although it was only 6:45pm. I finally made a call to Tom, saying that both tanker crews were safe, but that all eight of us were in the Yarck main tanker and that we had had to leave tanker 2 behind. Tom's only reply was, "I am just so relieved to hear from you!" We made it down Main Street only to find another big tree over the road at the caravan park blocking our way through. Now we were really trapped. We stopped and looked around for a safe way out. We had precious little time to assess our options as the fire was bearing down on us. A man suddenly appeared from nowhere and suggested that we try and push our way through the caravan park to another road and that he would follow us. We decided to try this, as most of the town was burning by now. We barged our way through two fences and a few trees, ploughed through the park, finally got back onto the road and headed for Buxton. We'd just made it!

THE FIRE WAS ALREADY THREATENING THE PERIMETER OF BUXTON

As we were leaving Marysville, the wind was extreme and boughs were coming down everywhere. The smoke was incredibly thick and dark as we slowly picked our way through the debris. The safe areas we had identified on our way into Marysville were now unfindable due to the extremely poor visibility. Finally we reached Buxton and could see again. There we asked if there were any safe areas and if any first aid or medical assistance were available. We were told however, that it would be best to head for Alexandra as the fire was already threatening the perimeter of Buxton. It seemed as though this fire wasn't going to give up easily! We made final contact with Tom advising him of our plans and when we got to Alexandra at 8:30pm, we got three crew members to hospital for medical treatment. Then we headed home to Yarck.

I got home at 11:00pm to find the family all outside looking after the house, as embers were coming down in our direction by now. I had a bite to eat then tried to get some sleep while the rest of the family took turns keeping watch on the property during the night.

Even weeks after the fires, I am still thanking our lucky stars that we survived and feeling very much for others who lost everything. Our special thanks goes to that resident who assisted us in picking a path through the Marysville caravan park and got us back onto the road, thus escaping the firestorm that seemed to be relentlessly pursuing us. We were amazingly fortunate to get out alive!

Photo: HWT

0.1 CALLING 000 PROVED HOPELESS AT THIS PHONE BOOTH.

0.2 STEAVENSON FALLS PARKING AREA BECOMES A SCENE OF DEVASTATION.

Photo: HWT

0.3 THE RAGING FIRES LEFT THIS HOUSE AND MINI IN RUINS.

0.4 NOTHING'S LEFT AT NARBETHONG'S ONLY PETROL STATION.

The sorry sight of another devastated Marysville household.

A MARYSVILLE
POLICEMAN'S DUTY

A LONE POLICE CAR RUSHES ONTO THE MARYSVILLE OVAL AND ORDERS PEOPLE TO LEAVE IMMEDIATELY.

"Go go, you must go now" screamed one of the Police officers from the car. They themselves had just driven through from Alexandra on the only road into Marysville that fateful afternoon. With the fire blazing on the ridge above the road in, neither of the two Police officers knew if they would make it into Marysville or what they would find if they did!

Once in Marysville they alerted as many residents in houses and visitors that they saw in the town to flee and flee fast. "Take the Marysville Buxton road and go for your lives, but you must go now!"

Once they thought their duty was done, they briefly stopped at the CFA station to see if everybody was all right. Check the oval they were told, there may be townsfolk there! So they gunned it down the road thinking they will drive past the oval on their way out to Alexandra.

The oval was full of people, waiting and wondering what to do! The trees were exploding in balls of fire around one side of the oval by this stage and the smoke was building in intensity. The wind was blowing at cyclone strength as that lone Police car drove on and ordered people to get in their cars and follow them.

They headed up onto the Marysville Buxton road and led up to 200 people out from the burning inferno that was by this stage engulfing Marysville. With the fear in their stomachs that the road ahead may already be blocked by fire or they may well become trapped by falling trees, they urged the people on!

Along the way they also evacuated other people from houses and buildings before finally arriving at Buxton and again had to push onto Alexandra as Buxton itself came under attack.

The police car roars onto Marysville oval warning residents to flee.

**WITHOUT MEN LIKE THESE,
MANY MORE MAY HAVE PERISHED THAT DAY.**

0.1 The famous Marysville Patisserie, gutted and destroyed.

0.2 Looking like a bomb had struck... the firestorm leaves its mark.

Photo: HWT

Photo: HWT

Repent Ye Come to the Lord
While yet there is time

The LORD giveth The LORD Taketh Away
BLESSED be the name of The LORD

GIPPSLAND
ABLAZE

THERE IS A RIVER CALLED THE BUNYIP WHICH RUNS DOWN FROM THE GREAT DIVIDE THROUGH THE WOODED HILLS OF WEST GIPPSLAND BEFORE LAZILY WINDING ITS WAY THROUGH THE SWAMPS OF KOO WEE RUP TO EMPTY ITSELF INTO WESTERN PORT BAY.

The swamps are drained now but once its waterholes and marshland concealed the lair of that fearsome Australian relative of the Loch Ness monster - the Bunyip, from which the river took its name. Aboriginal legends and sightings by early settlers told of this dark creature with fiery eyes that lurked in the billabongs and swamps ready to prey on any that might upset them.

0.1 FIREFIGHTERS STRUGGLED TO KEEP THE FIREFRONT AT BAY DUE TO THE STRONG WINDS THAT PREVAILED.

0.2 EVERY EFFORT WAS MADE TO PREVENT THESE SMALLER FIRES BECOMING MEGAFIRES.

0.3 SKYS ARE FILLED WITH DENSE GREY SMOKE AS EUCALYPTUS TREES BURN.

0.4 A FIRE TRUCK AND ITS CREW PREPARE FOR THE WORST AS FIRE LEAPS INTO THE AIR.

Photo: HWT

BUNYIP STATE PARK
LABERTOUCHE

BUNYIP STATE PARK

LABERTOUCHE

MELBOURNE 72KM

Drouin West

Princess Fwy

Princes Fwy

BUNYIP

Longwarry

Drouin

Drouin

For many years the little town of Bunyip on the west bank was the end of the road, where men left their drays and wagons to proceed eastwards towards Moe on foot or horseback.

From the mid 1800's this heavily forested area extending northwards into the mountains became the home of a thriving timber industry and little settlements sprang up which remain today. Gembrook, Noojee, Powelltown, Tonimbuk, Labertouche and Jindivick all date back to those times. Extensive forestry activity continued until as recently as 1992 when a large part of the area north of Bunyip was declared a state park and the sound of the chainsaw was replaced by the raucous call of the Yellow Tailed Black Cockatoo.

The Bunyip State Park provides many pleasant drives and walks through vegetation ranging from the tea- trees of the heathland to Banksias and vast stands of Silvertop, Messmate and the towering Mountain Ash- the tallest tree in the world after the Californian Redwood.

THE FIRE OF 2009

The years preceding the summer of 2008/09 had been relatively dry and the undergrowth and fallen debris in the forests were in a tinder dry state. People were apprehensive. They knew this huge amount of fuel and the hot, dry and windy weather provided the ideal conditions for a fire. No one could tell where it would start, nor when it would finish, but everyone knew that all that was required was a spark.

It is suspected that this spark was provided by a lightning strike on the Bunyip Track in the Park on Wednesday 4th February. The steep forested hills proved an unequal battlefield, providing ideal conditions for the fire, but at the same time making it extremely difficult for the fire fighting teams to combat them. By 4:00pm on Black Saturday the fire broke through containment lines out of the State Park forest and the ground crews retreated to concentrate their main effort to protect villages and property. The high winds were driving the fire toward the townships of Labertouche, Buln Buln, Tonimbuk and Drouin West and it had already destroyed twelve houses in its path.

Fire trucks came in from all over the state and even cement mixer vehicles were called on to be used as emergency tankers. The dedicated way the CFA and other agencies went about their mission was an inspiration to those battling to defend their properties. With tankers on the ground and

"Elvis" – the water bomber helicopter from above, the men of the CFA fought day and night

They gave practical advice to persons defending their own properties; simple but important things like telling them to change dangerous polyester clothing, liable to melt in the intense heat, to wool or cotton and advising them to drink at least a litre of water an hour to prevent dehydration- something that might not be thought of in the adrenaline charged heat of the battle.

This fire was fiercer than any the fighters had seen, just as severe as the other major fires that day and although it was finally contained on Monday the 9th February, it revived its ferocity with high winds the next day and was only eventually extinguished by soaking rains about three weeks after it began, having destroyed about 25 000 hectares of land.

That there was no loss of life was amazing, a miracle actually. The general manager of the CFA, Peter Schultz said it could be because the fire started in the uninhabited State Park and had given them some days warning prior to breaking out under the terrible conditions on Black Saturday.

The CFA had held five meetings and dropped letters in mailboxes to raise awareness so people had had more time to prepare.

THE FUTURE

The Bunyip fire on Black Saturday was caused by natural occurances, as have most others in the past, for example through lightning. The native flora shows remarkable resilience. Fire actually stimulates regrowth from under the bark of trees and germinates seed in the soil to start the cycle of re-growth and competition for light and nutrients between species to reach the final balanced stage of maturation.

As vegetation re-grows so too the animals return from surrounding areas. Even in the Park some survived. Park officials were thrilled to find twelve birds from a small colony of the critically endangered Helmeted Honeyeater had survived the fire, one of only two colonies in the world. The fire had stopped only 300 metres from their occupied habitat.

Wallabies, wombats and goannas will be seen again during the day and possums, bats, owls and gliders will be about at night. If you keep very still you might even see the glowing eyes of the bunyip near the river. Don't count on it though.

THE FIRE BROKE THROUGH THE CONTAINMENT LINES!

0.1

0.1 Glen Cromie Caravan Park cowers under the merciless flames.
0.2 Fierce winds, fierce fire, courageous firefighters.

0.2

Photo: HWT

GET OUT! GET OUT! GET OUT!

BILL HILL
Labertouche

The CFA briefed us on Friday at the Labertouche Hall. They told us at that meeting: Saturday would be a day of extreme heat, something we had never experienced before with temperatures of up to 50°C. There would be gale force winds and the fire would be so intense, there would be no way a person could ever outrun it. They advised anyone wanting to leave their homes to do so there and then, just don't leave it until Saturday. That was the message everyone got in this valley. I came away thinking that they were just trying to frighten us. But what happened?

EVERY SINGLE THING THEY MENTIONED IN THAT MEETING HAPPENED!!

There were fires already burning in the Bunyip State Park which had been started by lightning strikes and were still alight in inaccessible valleys.

When Saturday morning came, my youngest son, Tom, and I were home together. My wife was in Brisbane as her father wasn't well and she had gone up to see him. I was stuck there with just Tom, so I decided to call Nick, my eldest son, to come up from Melbourne for the day. I could tell by the tone of his voice he didn't really want to come because he had things to do in Melbourne, but out of family loyalty he came.

At about 11:30am, I got a phone call from 3AW asking what I was going to do. I said, "Stay, of course! There's no option here, we are on top of a hill, lots of cleared land around, and the flats have been cut three times with hay and silage. The wind is going to blow the fire down the Bunyip River (which it did), then turn around to the southwest. It is going to burn back over this direction, but it will have to go over all that dried out country that has got no feed on it, so we will just stand here and put it out with the garden hose." That's what I thought!

We were there waiting and it was getting hotter and hotter and, honestly, when I saw the fire, it was travelling like an express train down the Bunyip River! We were waiting for it to come back. At that stage I actually felt a bit guilty that I had brought Nick up, because it looked like he was going to be wasting his time. Anyway, we drove over to the neighbour's property, on the next hill to where we are, to get a different perspective of the fire. We could see the strength of it from that vantage point, and then Nick said, "We'd better get back and see if our place is all right, in case there are a few embers in the area."

As we drove up our driveway, suddenly before our eyes, a piece of ground as big as a football field burst into flame as if from nowhere. One minute it was grass, next minute it was a flaming mass! As we watched, it jumped to the next paddock, nothing in between, no trail, just another spot jump and from there, seconds later, into the forest. Some of the trees there are 120 feet high and the whole lot just caught alight from the top to the bottom and took off like a rocket. It would have been doing 95 kilometres per hour - no exaggerating! It went along at tremendous speed in front of us, and we could hear its horrendous roar!

"BILLY, GET OUT OF THE ROAD!! BILLY, GET OUT OF THE ROAD!!!!"

I still wasn't particularly worried at this stage because it had already gone through that area, and I literally thought the fire would burn itself out. I was over in the back paddock on the tractor, hosing out a fair sized grass fire with the fire pump when my son suddenly starting yelling out, "BILLY, GET OUT OF THE ROAD!! BILLY, GET OUT OF THE ROAD!!!!" Finally he was almost hysterical; this was a grown man in his 30's, not just a kid. He was yelling, "GET OUT! GET OUT! GET OUT!"

I looked over my shoulder and here was this GREAT INFERNO coming up the hill towards me, travelling at over 100 kilometres per hour, 20 metres high, and more than 50 metres wide, just going for it, all in one hit!! The fire was just swirling around, flashing and crackling. I was sitting on the tractor and I remember putting my hand up to my face and saying, "STOP! STOP!" It got to within half an inch of me and I don't know whether the tractor got me through or whether the fire just changed direction at that point. Had I been caught in the fire I would not be here today. If I had jumped off the tractor and tried to run, I would have tripped on the rough ground and certainly perished.

I WAS JUST COVERED IN BLISTERS, MY ARMS, MY LEGS, EVERYWHERE!

As soon as I got clear of the flames, all the burns blew up all over me immediately; I was just covered in blisters, my arms, my legs, everywhere. The flames never actually touched me; it was the radiant heat that caused all my burns. I got off the tractor and immersed myself completely in a nearby cattle trough. I then went to the house and by this stage I was getting a bit sore, so Nick suggested I go and get some help. I said "No, I'll be all right." I had blisters as big as ten and twenty cent pieces covering my arms completely, there would have been about 60 or more of them, as well as on my face. I thought, "If I could put some cream on them, I'll be right by the morning." The pain on my arms was getting pretty bad by this stage, so I got into the shower fully clothed to keep cool. When I got out I must have looked quite a mess, as Nick just said to Tom, "There's the keys, drive him straight to the Labertouche Hall."

THROUGH A WALL OF FLAME

When we took off to the hall, things were still burning all around us, and we were not sure where the fire had gone. I thought it had gone past us.

We came across a fire truck, and they offered to drive us to the hall. However another tanker came over to assist us. It was Drouin West tanker.

We were told to follow their tanker down Labertouche Rd, and one of Drouin West's crew offered to drive our car and they would escort us to safety. We proceeded down Labertouche Rd at about 20 kilometres per hour an hour, as there were trees down and fire was everywhere.

As we rounded the corner on Labertouche North Rd, it was clear that conditions had become perilous. Both sides of the road were surrounded by 20 feet flames, with the fire closing in. Conditions were very dangerous. However, we felt safe knowing that we were following Drouin West tanker. I know now, that if we had travelled down the road by ourselves, we would have died in the fire. It was that bad. The crew from Drouin West got us to the hall safely.

After arriving at the hall, the crew from Drouin West handed us over to another bloke, who was the Sector Commander, and much to my disappointment there was no-one there with any medical knowledge whatsoever.

One bloke looked at me and said, "You'll be right, mate! It looks a bit sore. If you go inside, we will put it in water for you." They found some ice, but the cold of the ice, and the pain was unbearable!! The smoke level in the hall was quite heavy, so they told me to lie on the floor. By this stage my legs were shaking, my arms were swollen, and my face was a mess. I said, "If I lie down on the floor mate, I will never get up again."

I have since learnt, that while we were in the hall, the crew from Drouin West stayed outside, and battled fires all around the hall, and saved it, as well as the Labertouche fire station. If it had not been for these guys, the hall may have been destroyed, and all of us inside could have been killed.

There was an ambulance waiting out on the highway for me, but they wouldn't let it come to us, so someone then escorted us out to the ambulance.

We got to the BP garage, and there was a doctor there who had some painkillers with him, so he gave me an injection to settle the pain. By that stage the medics had come, and they were about to put me in the helicopter when they got an emergency call to Port Phillip Bay. So they put me in an ambulance, and away we went. I had the sirens on all the way. The ambo said, "I'm not putting the sirens on because you are going to die; I just want to get you there as soon as we possibly can. The sooner you get there, the sooner you will get better."

There I was, sitting up in the ambulance, and they had me drugged as much as they could, when we came to a steep hill. The ambulance had to stop abruptly for something, and as it suddenly stopped, the gate came off the trolley, and it hit the back door with a thump. I thought, this is going to be funny! Here am I in a pair of jocks and socks, and nothing else, and I could just envisage myself shooting out the door and off down the hill, with the ambulance man chasing me!!!

Well, we finally got to the Alfred Hospital, and everything there seemed to be in a complete silence. It was only pointed out to me recently, when the medical staff said, "Did you notice anything unusual about the hospital that day?" Hospitals are normally fairly busy places with people rushing everywhere, but on this particular day there was nothing but silence. It was quite eerie!! Quite a few people were coming in from the fires, and the hospital didn't know how many more to expect. They had been advised of the fires in the Kinglake area, and there was obviously no knowing what lay ahead.

THEY BURST ALL THE BLISTERS

They wrapped my hands up in Glad Wrap. I didn't know whether they were going to put me in a microwave or what they were going to do to me! They burst all the blisters which I thought was interesting, because I had always been taught to leave them. This is actually part of the procedure; they get a scrubbing brush and scrub all the skin, completely scrub it all, to clean it.

I said "Can I go now, seeing as you've done all you can do?"

"Give me some ointment to put on, and I will go." They told me that I would be there for a day or two and I replied, "I'm not stopping here, the place has been burnt out at home, I've got work to do back there, and I've got to get home to do it. It's getting close to midnight and I'm getting jolly tired." They told me they were going to put me in the ward. I really didn't think I needed to stay overnight in the hospital, and kept asking when I could leave. On Tuesday, they finally unwrapped my burns, and when I saw them I said, "Perhaps I will stay here for a couple of days!"

Three weeks later I was still there. I had to have a huge patch of skin taken off my leg, and grafted onto my arm. My leg was red raw where they had taken the skin off, and probably gave me more pain than my arm.

AWESOME CARE, THEY COULDN'T DO ENOUGH FOR ME!

What an amazing job the medical staff did! I never felt any pain from the time I got into the Alfred Hospital, until the time I left. I was probably drugged a fair bit at different times, but I was always coherent. I suppose, apart from the plastic surgeon, the pain management team were the most important in the whole healing process. The first day I had to have a bath, and I wasn't looking forward to the skin going into hot water, but no, they fixed it up so there was no pain whatsoever. The expertise and the professional result of every particular team can't be described; it was very, very good. As they took the wraps off over the next few days, the skin started to peel, and the nurses would spend hours and hours with a pair of scissors and tweezers, just cutting off little bits of skin. Head nurses would come in, nurses who hadn't actually nursed on a day to day ward for years, and cut away this skin, just to get me right. I came out with skin like a baby. Awesome care, they couldn't do enough for me! Everything I needed was there.

There were other things that happened behind the scenes that I wasn't aware of. I had always been a pretty independent sort of a person and not the sort to ask for help, so I was really amazed that all this could happen without me even requesting it. All my phone calls and visitors were vetted, so I could heal as quickly as possible.

You could say I was unlucky, because I got burnt, but I consider myself lucky, as I am still alive. I suppose I was stupid, because I put myself in a position I shouldn't have been in, not realizing the dangers. I thought I was doing the right thing at that time, but the fire moved so FAST, it was absolutely unpredictable!

NANNETTE GERRARD
Bunyip

Mrs. Gerrard was home with her invalid husband and her daughter who has a studio on the property. We were on fire-alert and I thought I knew about fires as I had I lived in Erica for years where they were a threat many times. We were prepared with our mops, buckets and hoses all at hand. We were very calm.

We could see the smoke in the air and at 2:30pm our neighbours sent us a text message to advise us that we were about to get some embers. So we got ready, still calm. We have a tower here and my daughter could see a long way. We got my husband out of the house (he has a heart condition) and got the dogs inside. We were still very calm, just waiting for spot fires.

A young man, Michael, arrived and helped us fix and connect our hoses and then he just hung around. He lives in Warragul, but didn't feel easy about going home and I couldn't persuade him to go. At about 3:00pm the wind changed and we started getting embers. We had been watching the flames and smoke across at Jindivick and the fire was moving away from us.

Suddenly our neighbour texted: "Look to the front of your property, you have two seconds to prepare yourselves!" My daughter organised us - we split into two groups and went to our stations. God had sent that young man, Michael to us and he hadn't felt able to leave us. Then another friend arrived. My post was in the front of the house so I was on the perimeter waiting.

Then it came, roaring up the paddock from behind us. A great rolling wall of fire tumbling like a long barrel, with the noise of 1200 bulldozers all at once. The noise was terrific - we were shouting at the top of our voices. Andrew and I were filling buckets to protect the perimeter of the house.

"GOD HELP US! DO SOMETHING! WE LOVE YOU!"
My daughter and our friend were at the other side of the house. The fire was raging all around us - it came to within a metre of our garden and all the paddocks were on fire. My hair was singed and my scarf wrapped around my face was scorched.

By this time I was on my knees calling out, "God help us! Do something! We love you!" The fire then turned and went down to the lake.

Our friend called out, "Tell Him we need some rain, and send it now!" So I called out, "Lord, send us rain, and send it now!"

The rain came, it was like when you drop a hose and it snakes along the ground - the rain came spurting down like silver streaks of water through the air. That helped us and we knew then we would be OK.

As the fire passed we came back together - it felt like we'd just come back from a battlefield.

MIRACULOUS
DELIVERANCE!

MRS. GERRARD OF DROUIN WEST TELLS HER STORY
OF FAITH IN GOD AND A MIRACULOUS DELIVERANCE
ON SATURDAY 7TH FEBRUARY.

YOU HAVE TWO SECONDS TO PREPARE YOURSELVES!

Important message to all
Trail Bike Riders
and Four Wheel Drivers

Here it comes…! The smoke tells the intensity of the fire which lies behind bush land yet to be consumed.

MAYBE WE WEREN'T READY TO GO?

The young men said, "We could hear you shouting out to God, above the noise of the roaring fire." Now I'm a softly spoken person - I don't generally have the strength for volume in my voice. I'm 72, and I've never experienced anything like it before. Never been so close to dying. We praised the Lord and thanked God; maybe we weren't ready to go?

Right around the house is a ring untouched by the fire; the house and rose garden looked as though nothing has happened. The white wooden fence is there, but it is untouched. The fire burnt the foliage and the ferns under the fence; outside the fence all the native trees and the conifers are gone - totally burnt.

Our neighbour had cows in the next paddock and as the fire roared on, my daughter said, "I'm going to bring the cows over." She was amazing. She brought them over to our sand area where we had some horses. When the horses saw the cows, they helped her with the roundup.

I said, "Look at that!" The horses had the cows in a ring, just calmly grazing the perimeter around them so that the cows couldn't get out. The animals were so calm – they must have felt the Lord's hand over them.

"LORD, GIVE ME THE STRENGTH OF TWENTY MEN!"

At one stage I was riding the motor bike. I nearly crashed many times, as I couldn't see more than ten feet in front and sure enough – I turned the bike over. I said, "Lord, give me the strength of twenty men!" I put my leg on the upturned bike and over it came. Later, my daughter found blood on the back of my head and on my arm.

I can't say it was frightening – it was an experience we were carried through. My faith is strong; I don't start the day unless I ask the Lord if I am doing His will. He protected us as if He put a cone over us and said, "I will protect you." He sent us a guardian angel to protect us. Michael was like an angel and he said later that he didn't know why he stayed. The other young man was sent to us too. My husband is not well; we couldn't have done it on our own. We were just calling above the noise, "Lord, God help us!" Our voices went above the noise of the fire, even though we could hardly breathe. I've had a cough ever since.

I'M SURE ALL THESE DISASTERS ARE TO BRING US TO GOD

If you believe in God and put your life in His hand, He'll be with you. I'm sure all these disasters are to bring us to God. All these disasters overseas, in lands where very few are living with God, are surely a sign of the end of times. I feel I live in the world, but I'm not of it. I got on my knees and said, "Please, Lord, I want you to save my family. I'm 72, but these young people…."

WE JUST PRAISE THE LORD THAT WE WERE ALL PRESERVED.

0.1   Firefighters contemplate the grim task ahead of them.

0.2   Strong winds create a frenzy of flame and fireballs.

0.3   Helpless, this holiday cabin waits to be engulfed.

Fire crews do all they can on the fire near Bunyip State Park bushfire.   0.4

DSE crews bulldoze vital containment lines.

MARK KNIGHT

Tonimbuk

DRAWING ON
EXPERIENCE!

THE BUSHFIRES THAT CUT A SWATHE ACROSS VICTORIA IN FEBRUARY THIS YEAR WERE ONE OF OUR COUNTRY'S WORST NATURAL DISASTERS. PEOPLE AROUND AUSTRALIA, AND INDEED THE REST OF THE WORLD, WERE WITNESS TO THE CATASTROPHE THROUGH THEIR TELEVISIONS, NEWSPAPERS, RADIOS AND ON THE INTERNET.

As an editorial cartoonist for a Melbourne newspaper, the Herald Sun, I often draw about events that affect the lives of Victorians. This is usually done from the comfort of my desk at our Southbank offices.

My coverage of these bushfires, however, would be a new experience in cartooning on an issue. I found myself cartooning on the frontline of a major event. The work of the great WW1 artist Will Dyson always inspired me for its powerful imagery, and at the same time amazed me as to how he could work amongst such calamities. I was soon to gain an insight.

My family and I live about 90 kilometres east of the city, on a series of dirt roads called Tonimbuk, situated on the edge of the Bunyip State Park. My wife Sophy and I made the tree change about 14 years ago, to pursue our love of horses, have a family, and take in a bit of serenity.

FIRE IS A CONSTANT COMPANION!

However, when you live on the edge of nearly 17,000 hectares of eucalypt forest, fire is a constant companion. During our time in Tonimbuk we have faced several major fires, but none had come so close as to seriously imperil our property. We have also observed our local climate changing. Winters were drier, and the summers harsher. Local creeks that once flowed all year, now run dry in January. The threat of a major fire episode was increasing.

So as another Victorian summer approached, we believed we had done all we could do to prepare ourselves, and hoped Mother Nature would do her bit, and look kindly upon us. Sadly, she did not.

It didn't rain in January. We watched the world's best tennis players melt on centre court in Melbourne during the Australian Open, enduring several days of temperatures above 45°C. Before our eyes the landscape faded to a yellowish brown, and trees with a European heritage threw their leaves down in surrender to the great southern land's unblinking glare.

LIGHTNING STRIKES

On Monday the 2nd of February, it seemed there might be some relief, when thunderstorm clouds gathered over the ranges behind us. It brought some rain, but we were to pay a high price for the paltry 5mm in the bottom of the rain gauge. Lightning strikes started several small fires in a valley of the Bunyip State Park, five kilometre to our north. Driving up to the top of the ridge, I could see the small trail of white smoke drift out of the forest in the valley below. At the same time the weather bureau was predicting that the coming Saturday would see temperatures in excess of 45°C, with winds of over 100 kilometres per hour. It didn't look good.

So in the days ahead, we went about preparing ourselves for what might eventuate that weekend. I spent the week drawing cartoons about the beginning of the new Federal parliamentary session, and Kevin Rudd's $42 billion stimulus package. With one eye on a very exciting start to the political year, and the other eye on the looming smoke cloud over the ridge, they combined in one cartoon with Wayne Swan piloting Elvis the water-bombing helicopter. He is depicted dumping a payload of cash on the electorate. At least I was getting some value out of these fires.

By Friday, the children, wife, livestock and other precious items were trucked out to safety. Attending a CFA meeting that morning in Labertouche, the warnings were loud and clear, that if the predicted winds eventuated, the Bunyip fire would take off and head our way like an express train.

THAT EERIE ORANGE LIGHT CAST BY THE SUN'S RAYS

When Saturday the 7th of February dawned there was a surreal calm before the storm. Anyone who lives in bushfire prone areas knows well that eerie orange light cast by the sun's rays when filtered through the smoke of a bushfire. It has a beautiful but unsettling luminosity.

The hot stillness was broken by the baritone thud of the two Erickson Air-crane helicopters, as they resumed their bombardment of the fire in a last ditch attempt to tame it. I drove the kilometre down the road to where they were flying out of a neighbour's paddock. These leviathans, affectionately named Elvis and Bluey, attract a crowd wherever they go. They are the closest thing we have to The Thunderbirds and International Rescue. I stood with a few locals and watched the awesome display, feeling somewhat

THE SCENE AT TONIMBUK, VICTORIA, SATURDAY 7th FEB 2009. THANKS TO THE BRAVE DSE CREWS WHO CAME FROM NOWA NOWA, ROSEBUD AND MELBOURNE AND GOOD MATE DAVE WHO SAVED MY HOME AND QUITE POSSIBLY MY LIFE.... Knight

OH OH

THE VICTORIAN BUSHFIRES WERE EQUIVALENT TO 1500 HIROSHIMA ATOMIC BOMBS — REPORT

comforted that we had these heavy hitters involved in the fight.

As if on cue at midday, and as predicted, the hot northerly winds arrived. We watched as the smoke cloud over the hill turned from white, to brown, to black, mushrooming skyward. I arrived back home to be greeted by a mate who had decided to come up and help me with any potential fire. Dave was once a Tonimbuk resident and a good man to have in your trench when things got hot. He was carrying another fire fighting pump and hose, which on Black Saturday was akin to a friend turning up with a slab of your favourite beer under his arm. He was very welcome.

THE MOUNTAIN HAD EXPLODED IN FLAME
By now the mountain had exploded in flame, goaded by huge winds and high temperatures. We stood and watched as the conflagration spread across our tree topped horizon, the smoke cloud now a dark, voluminous, churning monster towering over us.

Then the cavalry arrived. Two white utes carrying Department of Sustainability and Environment (DSE) fire fighters from the Nowa Nowa branch arrived. They were joined by crews from Melbourne and Rosebud and the Bunyip CFA. We weren't alone! The team leader inspected our equipment, checked how much water we had, (our pool was about to justify its installation expense), and whether we were mentally ready for the fight. The verdict was that our property offered a good clearing for fire units to operate out of, and they would stay and defend us.

I RESISTED A STRONG URGE FOR A MAN HUG AT THAT POINT.
Then roles were assigned. Dave and I were given the job of protecting the house with our fire pumps. The crews would take care of the rest. Then we waited for the fire to come down to us through the forest as the mercury hit 46°C.

The waiting is the hardest part. Our dirt road had become the Hindenburg Line. It was where an attempt would be made to stop the fire's progress south. At this point the fire was also trying to do our heads in, with the towering cumulonimbus smoke clouds creating their own thunder. It was then I had a moment of hesitation about what I had gotten myself into. Standing next to me, a fireman with a huge grin asked if I could take the mickey out of one of his crew in a cartoon. "Now?" I said incredulously, but the humour was a welcome distraction.

THE ROAR OF 1,000 V8 ENGINES
The fire arrived late that afternoon with the roar of 1,000 V8 internal combustion engines revving in anger, sucking in oxygen and spewing out exhaust gases and sparks. It catapulted embers like incendiary bombs ahead of its march forward, which, upon landing in parched paddocks instantly gave birth to the fire's progeny. Fire crews raced to these and put them out. Tea trees exploded, igniting tree canopies as a wind change whipped things up again. Now, with fire hose in hand, all I cared about was doing what Mother Nature had failed to do...make it rain on the house for the next twenty minutes as the firefront passed.

By 3:00am on Sunday morning the fire finally relented, and was deemed under control. The blackness of the bush that night was punctuated with thousands of red fire-lit fairy lights. The stillness was in contrast to the day's events, where amongst the chaos, our swimming pool filled tankers like a petrol station pumps gas, our hayshed was miraculously saved, and my wife Sophy appeared out of nowhere to happily see our house still standing and to offer support and a coldie. We sat on the verandah and watched an orange glow rise in the distance as the fire sadly consumed

a neighbour's house a kilometre away, sometime after midnight. Then I caught a few hours sleep ...with one eye open.

I HAD TO DRAW A CARTOON FOR THE NEXT DAY'S PAPER
In the early dawn, I awoke to a landscape resembling the moon with trees. That smell of charcoal would be with me for life I thought, as I walked through smouldering remains. It was not until fire crews departed later that Sunday morning, that I realised I had to draw a cartoon for the next day's paper. I went into my studio and sat down at the computer and caught up with what had happened in other parts of the state. I read of the horror of Callignee, Kinglake and Marysville. I rang our news desk and told them I would draw something for that night's edition, but just what that was, I wasn't quite sure. I was exhausted and filthy but I was still running on adrenalin. This was a tragic yet historic event, and I felt it important to put my experience on the record. I hoped the drawing would convey to readers what people on the firefront were going through. It was also good therapy. I needed to unload, so why not do it on paper. I didn't know where to start, the story was so big, so I simply told my story in a thank you letter to those fire crews and friend Dave, who helped save my bacon on Black Saturday. The figures in the cartoon are a scribble. I had lost my usual draughtsmanship, but the wild Bruce Petty-ish energy in this sketch said it better than something more precise. The colour in the drawing, a wash of reds oranges and yellows, looks like it has been hosed on by the CFA. The cartoon has the look and feel of something drawn on the frontline. Indeed the desk where I drew it is only 30 metres from where the fires finished up.

Many of the early drawings reflected the solemnity of the huge loss of life. I made comparisons between this disaster and the global financial crisis. But just as the burnt stringybarks sprout new green shoots, the humour in my drawings began to re-emerge. A cartoon on Sam the koala drinking a CFA unit dry or Prime Minister Kevin Rudd offering "Free Hugs" at a fire refuge brought a smile to readers' faces.

AND BY HECK, WE NEEDED A LAUGH ALMOST AS MUCH AS WE NEEDED SOME RAIN.

0.1 Crown fires rush through the tops of the trees devouring large swathes of the Bunyip State Forest.

0.2 The aircrane pilot observes the firefront from the relative safety of the cockpit.

0.1

0.2

Photo: HWT

153 FIRESTORM

0.1 The fire breaks out of the Bunyip State Park.
0.2 Weary fighters do their best to protect Labertouche properties.

Photo: Jason South

0.3 An exhausted fire captain.
0.4 A disheartened farmer takes in the devastation.

THE GARDEN OF VICTORIA
BURNS

SCATTERED AMONG THE OLD FORESTS AND PLANTATIONS OF THE ROLLING FOOTHILLS OF THE STRZELECKI RANGES, ARE SMALL PICTURESQUE TOWNS AND VILLAGES, THEIR SCENIC BEAUTY CONFIRMING THE OLD SAYING THAT "GIPPSLAND IS THE GARDEN OF VICTORIA."

A leisurely Saturday drive on the twisting roads through these hills takes one through places with intriguing names like Budgeree and Balook, Jumbuk and Jeeralang. Generous rainfall and fertile soils have combined to produce the lush forests and green paddocks that provide an idyllic setting for those who have chosen to live a country lifestyle in the bush. It was pretty close to paradise as far as the residents were concerned.

Among these places can be found Churchill, a university town of 5000 people, and Callignee, hardly a village, but rather a collection of neighbours living peacefully among the tall mountain ash and tree ferns. Other villages in the area include Hazelwood and Le Roy. These are names that would become etched in the memory of the nation as this great fire changed their paradise to something akin to hell.

Fire had always been a threat in these parts of course, but a threat that tended to fade in the mind, as summer after summer passed uneventfully. There had not been a major fire in the area for years. In these circumstances, Total Fire Ban days tend to become a routine, and the strange human thinking that 'It won't happen to me', often leads to a complacency that puts any danger far away. On the other hand, many understood that this hot, dry summer had been exceptional and could pose a very real threat to their property and their lives. They understood the risk and prepared as best they could for what might happen. But whether people were alert or complacent, there was nothing that could prepare them for the magnitude of the raging inferno that roared through the area on 7th February 2009, claiming 21 lives, and changing the lives of the survivors forever.

THIS CHAPTER TELLS THE STORIES OF THOSE WHO SURVIVED, AND THE BRAVERY OF THOSE WHO DID THEIR UTMOST TO HELP.

0.1 MELBOURNE'S POWER SUPPLY IS THREATENED AS SMOKE BILLOWS BEHIND HAZELWOOD POWER STATION.

0.2 ELECTRICITY IS CUT AS POWER LINES CRASH TO THE GROUND.

0.3 A HAY SHED ERUPTS INTO FLAMES EMITTING THICK ACRID SMOKE.

0.4 A DETERMINED FARMER STRIVES TO HALT THE BLAZE.

CHURCHILL, DELBURN
CALLIGNEE

Moe

Traralgon

Princes Fwy

Morwell

Princes Fwy

CALLIGNEE

DELBURN

MELBOURNE 136KM

CHURCHILL

THE INFERNO STARTED AT CHURCHILL!

It started at 1:30 pm in a pine plantation, only about a kilometre from the edge of Churchill. Fanned by the high winds that reached 120 kilometres per hour at times, the flames accelerated like an express train, heading in a south east direction towards Jeeralang, Jumbuk and Budgeree. The fire soon became an unstoppable conflagration of flame and smoke and heat; radiant heat so intense, that trees ahead exploded into flame, the volatile oils given off by their leaves providing the fuel to produce nature's own incendiary bombs. The noise was tremendous. People have described it as the noise of five jumbo jets taking off simultaneously.

The firefighters had no hope of stopping the juggernaut. At best they could try to contain it, help people to evacuate, and attempt where possible to protect property. About 400 firefighters poured into the area. The CFA, SES, DSE and Parks Victoria rushed their men and women to the rapidly extending battlefield, with reinforcements coming from as far afield as South Australia. The Monash University campus in Churchill was set up as a staging post.

The CFA men were already tired from fighting a large fire in the nearby Delburn area the day before, but as this was now contained, they willingly threw themselves into the battle again. With their lives constantly at risk, they fought for hours on end, snatching an occasional cat-nap when and where they could. Firebreaks were bulldozed through forests, but such was the force of the wind that burning embers were blown kilometres ahead, starting new spot fires.

THEN CALLIGNEE WAS ALL BUT DESTROYED!

The area worst hit was around Callignee, which was all but destroyed. Many persons in Callignee were unaware that the danger was so close. The fire had appeared to be passing them to the west, although as a precaution, many women and children evacuated to nearby Traralgon. Others stayed on, prepared to defend their homes whilst hoping the danger would pass. But around 6:00pm, the wind veered around, blowing now from the southwest, and within minutes a huge wall of flame and smoke roared over the hills toward them. A survivor who escaped just in time said the whole place seemed to catch alight simultaneously. For those who stayed a little longer, there was no way of getting out, as all escape routes were cut off by the fire. The ABC Radio aired the chilling message, "It is now too late to leave". Twenty one people perished that day. What remained was a black and white landscape, twisted metal sheets wrapped by the gale in their semi-molten state around blackened trees, molten glass from car windows, and fireplaces and chimneys standing as silent sentinels over the ashen piles of what people had once called their homes.

The devastation was huge. Fifty seven houses had been destroyed, and over 36,000 hectares of land was left desolate. The land will recover with time, trees will sprout again, and the wildlife will return, but the human cost can never really be counted. It was a day of tragedy for many families. Two

THE INFERNO

men came to help defend a relative's home in Callignee, and despite police warnings, they still went in. Their bodies were found in a metal bath tub they had tried to shelter in. There was no escape.

WAS IT ARSON?

It is terrible to think of the depraved mind that would deliberately start such a fire, but like many other fires over the years, forensic evidence showed that this killer fire was the work of an arsonist. A few weeks later they caught a man. If found guilty, he will face a sentence of 25 years or more in jail. While this can never compensate for the loss of loved ones, it is intended to act as a deterrent to others in future. Perhaps he never intended it to get as bad as it did. If so, what a foolish act of cruelty. There is no way anyone can control the smallest naked flame, in the windy conditions and temperature of 46°C that existed that day.

THE COMMUNITY RESPONSE

But if the fire was caused by the worst in human nature, it also brought out a wonderful response from the community, who rallied to help persons they had not known before. Donations as varied as clothing, canned food, cleaning products and farm tools, as well as offers of practical help poured in. Charities collected millions of dollars. Families were given temporary accommodation, and the Federal and State governments fulfilled their responsibilities to provide as much assistance as possible, to help set people on their feet again. It is wonderful the way a disaster can cause people to forget their own interests and get down to the things that matter. How many turned to God that day, who can say, but many persons who never even go to church have commented, 'I was aware Someone was watching over me from above'.

Even those that perished would have had moments to consider eternal realities. Almost every newspaper referred to the extremity of the fires as HELL ON EARTH!

THE FUTURE

These places will be rebuilt. Already there are foundations of new buildings emerging among the blackened trees. A carpet of fresh green grass has sprung up after the rain, some blackened trees that still had life in them are sprouting again, and brave survivors are piecing their lives together, but it will never be the same for them.

The memories of Black Saturday will be passed down the generations as a day of disaster and human depravity, a day of suffering and death, but also a day of bravery in the face of impossible odds, and of wonderful sympathy and support from total strangers. Many small acts of unselfishness, combined with the heroic deeds of those who risked their lives to save others, made it a day that will ever be remembered in the annals of Australia - Black Saturday, 7 February 2009.

Photo: HWT

Elvis the famous firefighting helicopter heads in as the fire incinerates the tinder dry bushland

0.1

0.1 Eucalyptus oil of the Australian gum trees provide deadly fuel for the all consuming fire.
0.2 Hungry for oxygen, fireballs erupt from a heavily burning bush land.

0.2

0.3 The sun's rays are blanketed by the deep smoky haze.

0.4 Property and vehicle owners were faced with utter devastation.

DAVID TREE
Churchill

THE KOALA MAN

WE WERE WORKING A STRIP OF CONTROLLED BURN UP SAMPSON'S ROAD. THIS IS A ROAD THAT RUNS EAST-WEST, FROM THE STRZELECKI HIGHWAY UP TO OLD THORPDALE ROAD.

An area was lit up, to burn back into the firefront that otherwise we couldn't get to. We had been working that area most of the day. It was early afternoon, and we were just coming up the road, when all of a sudden, we all said it about the same time, "There's a koala."

Having an absolutely uncontrollable passion for wildlife, I didn't even check with the officer in charge, I just pulled the truck over and bailed out. I remember saying something about, "Gotta go and see how he is going." So I bailed out of the fire truck, and the koala looked back and sort of walked a bit more, then it just sat and plonked.

The water thing, it just seemed like the right thing to do. Everything needs water at some stage. That was the only thing I thought, it's a universal food. So I yelled out for a bottle of water from the guys on the truck, and they threw me one. We always keep heaps of water on the truck. I just sort of tipped it up into my hand first, to pool it. On pooling the water, it obviously smelt it. So I dribbled it down the front of the bottle, and then it was just like a baby drinking a bottle. They seem to think that maybe the paw coming up, and resting in my hand with the cold water, might have given it some sort of pain relief. The tactile response regardless, was special!!! There is no doubt about it, it was really special.

It just seemed like the only thing to do. It was an instantaneous, totally uninstructed response to stop.

Mark Pardy, a DSE worker with us at the time, took the photos. Mark is the one to be credited, he was the one who had the foresight. He saw it and said, "That would make an amazing photo," not knowing the response ahead.

We then got an emergency call to go somewhere else, so we had to leave. I rang the rescue people, but they couldn't get in there straight away. When they did, they found the koala pretty much where I said it would be. It was then transported to Traralgon, then onto Rawson, where it received the care that it needed.

The thing to remember is that the media drove this. This is something that you could have had 50 million dollars in the bank, and you wouldn't be able to drive it. It was driven by the media, and supported by the public's opinion of it. It's quite pure and simple, it was a spur of the moment action, and I think that's the magical part of the photo.

THE RESCUE CREW NAMED HER SAMANTHA, AND SINCE, IT'S BEEN SHORTENED TO SAM, AS SHE WAS FOUND UP SAMPSON'S ROAD.

Photos: Picture Media

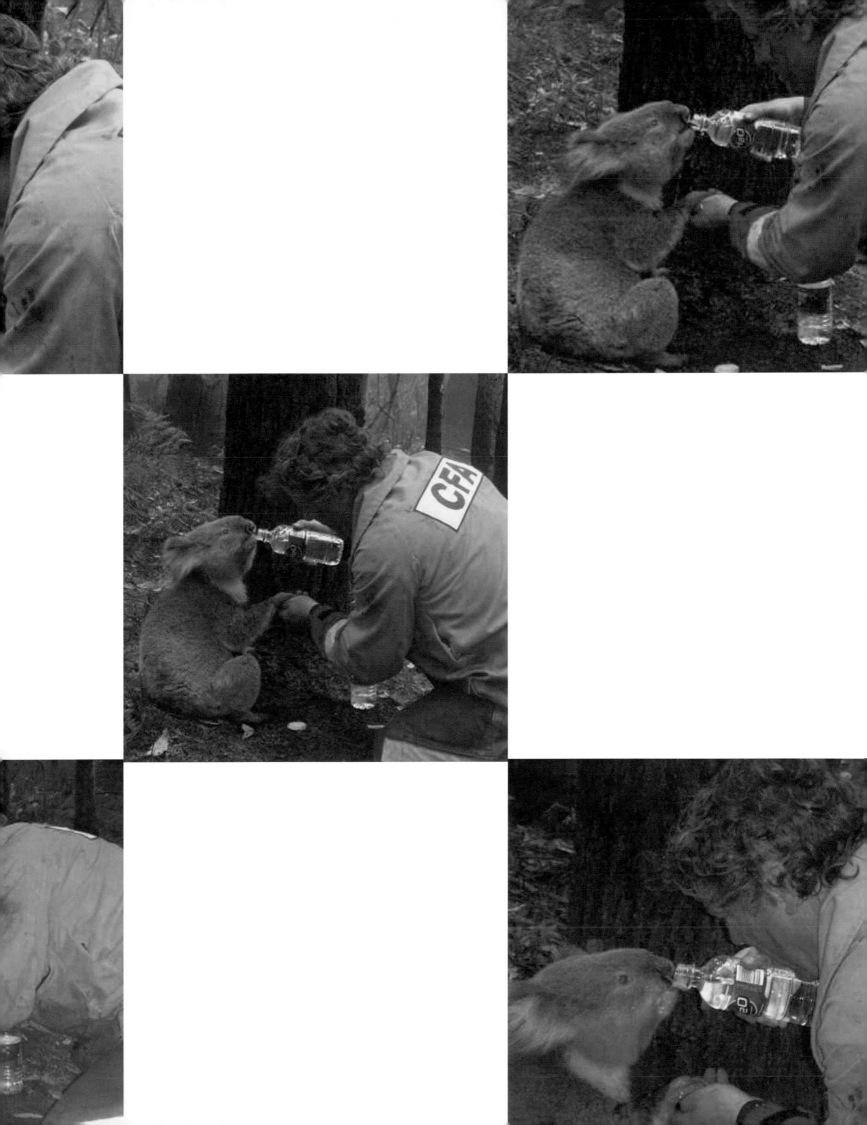

ANDREW KLEINIG &
GAVIN WIGGINTON

Callignee

BURNT TO THE
GROUND

ON THE DAY WHEN THE FIRE STORM STRUCK (7TH FEBRUARY), WE WERE AT OUR HOUSE READY TO DEFEND. BY MID AFTERNOON, THERE WAS HEAVY SMOKE ACROSS OUR PART OF GIPPSLAND FROM A FIRE 20 KILOMETRES AWAY.

We implemented our fire plan, which involved a whole set of things that we had previously rehearsed. In particular, we donned appropriate clothing, put the car in the shed, removed essential items from the house to the shed (including the computer on which I am now writing this story), hosed down the house, and undertook other preparatory works. Around 5:45pm, an eerie smoke and fog enveloped the area, and we could hear a deep rumbling noise approaching.

First, it started to grow very dark and we became the focus of a growing ember attack. We patrolled the area around the house putting out spot fires, then we noticed on the far horizon, that there was a bright glow on the ridge below our house, which turned to yellow, then orange, and finally red. By now, many trees around the house had caught alight and were burning, and there was a deafening roar all around us. We retreated into the house.

Then the fire storm arrived at the clearing, and hit the house. The flames were 100 feet high in the air, spread across a wide front, and travelling horizontally. From our vantage point, we realised that this was no ordinary fire. Apparently, from aerial imaging, the temperature of the fire reached up to 3000°C.

As we watched from inside the house, we could see the flames hitting the windows and spreading sideways. Then the glass started to crack. We retreated into the laundry at the back of the house, while Andrew had the water hose at the ready. The glass on the front of the house started to break, and the fire entered the house. Andrew tried to hose the flames but the water pump failed, due to lack of oxygen.

We stayed in the laundry for about ten minutes, lying on the floor and trying to get oxygen, as the solid floor heated up from flames beneath the house, and smoke started to get through the walls. By this stage I was close to losing consciousness from smoke inhalation and lack of oxygen, and remember saying that I couldn't breathe. At this point, Andrew called the evacuation, took my hand and led me out of the house down the back steps, which were already on fire. We sprinted across to the shed about six metres away, and Andrew put out a fire in the shed as I arrived. We slammed the roller doors closed and jumped into the car, where we lay down. By now, the firefront had passed through (it took around ten minutes), and the fire had now taken hold in the house.

THE HOUSE TOOK AROUND 15 MINUTES TO BURN TO THE GROUND

The flames from the house fire nearly cooked us in the shed, but miraculously the shed held firm, and we only stayed conscious by talking to each other. The temperature in the car was around 50°C + (on car thermometer). Suddenly, the side door of the shed, on the opposite side to the fire, popped out, allowing some oxygen to get to us. Then a fire started up inside the shed, so we got out of the car and extinguished the fire.

By this stage, the house had collapsed, and was fully gone. The fire having now subsided, we staggered out the side door of the shed. There was fire in the trees all around, but the radiant heat had reduced significantly. We could not believe that we were still alive.

Shortly after, our nearest neighbours arrived at our house, having survived their own inferno two kilometres up the road. Together, we walked the three kilometres down the hill to the village. There were trees blazing with fire on either side, while others had fallen and were still burning on the road. On both sides of the road we saw our neighbours' houses burning. The air was thick with smoke, and we were still struggling to breathe.

Miraculously, we arrived at the edge of the village, which had not been hit by the fire. People greeted us as we emerged through the smoke, amazed that we had survived the inferno.

0.1 A hilltop home, amidst the tall timbers, two years to build...
0.2 15 minutes to destruct!

0.1

0.2

0.1 Once a family home, now a mangled mess.
0.2 House and contents are destroyed by the ruthless firestorm.

0.1

0.2

0.3 Another home destroyed by the inferno that went through the Delburn area.

0.4 The utter destruction tells the story. . .

BENDIGO AND REDESDALE
ALIGHT

BENDIGO, ONE OF VICTORIA'S OLDEST CITIES, STARTED BACK IN THE 1850'S DURING THE GOLD RUSH DAYS AND GREW WITHIN A FEW YEARS FROM A GOLD MINER'S POPPET TO A THRIVING RICH CITY.

The population boomed until the gold became scarce, with many miners then leaving the city to turn their hands to more fruitful labour. Bendigo continued to grow and is steeped in heritage character, with many older buildings scattered through its sprawling suburbs. These suburbs reach out in all directions, but are concentrated around the diggings of the old gold rush days.

0.1 A PARKING LOT BECOMES A GRAVEYARD OF CHARRED VEHICLES.

0.2 CORRUGATED IRON BUCKLES IN THE HEAT.

0.3 SMOKE BILLOWS BEHIND ONE OF BENDIGO'S FAMOUS POPPET HEADS.

0.4 A MOTORIST FACED BY FLAMES.

BENDIGO
REDESDALE

BENDIGO

Mclvor Hwy

Calder Hwy

MELBOURNE 128KM

Lake
Eppalock

REDESDALE

The old diggings have become gullies of dense scrub, towering gum trees and thick native grasses with houses built all around it, and these pockets of bush were to prove a death trap for the city.

And so Black Saturday dawned on a city that had hardly ever been affected by bush fires before! Bendigo being an inland city had always known heat and low humidity, and so the extreme conditions of 7th February were not that much different from most other hot summer days.

By 11:00am the temperature had reached 40°C, and by midday it was in the mid 40's with the wind reaching well over sixty kilometres per hour.

About five kilometres north-west of the outer reaches of Bendigo, at about 3:30pm, somebody appears to have carelessly disposed of a cigarette butt out of a car window. On a day like this, it only takes the smallest thing to make the biggest thing happen, and so it did.

The fire spread slowly at first without attracting a huge amount of attention, and then the wind rose and whipped the fire into a frenzy, moving it at such a speed that people barely had time to leave their homes. The overgrown scrubby gullies acted as funnels to accelerate it towards the city of Bendigo.

The fire was not described as a wall of fire like other affected areas, but rather as a rolling fireball that ripped through Maiden Gully and Eaglehawk then on to Long Gully. Spreading rapidly, it caught the most off guard and people were forced to leave their homes and all their belongings when fleeing to safety! Police drove into streets screaming at people over their loud hailers to get out, and get out now!

Mercifully there was only one death in Long Gully, even though 57 homes were destroyed along with 500 hectares of land. The main difference between this fire and that of Kinglake and Marysville was the number of streets that lead away from the fire area which made it easier for residents to flee, although these became choked with sightseers as people flocked to view the inferno. The fire was finally checked just two kilometres from the city's centre.

REDESDALE

Redesdale is a farming area about half way between Kilmore and Bendigo that also was caught unawares on Black Saturday. A cluster of farm houses and rural acreage properties tucked into the rolling hills just south of Lake Eppalock came under sudden flame attack which was fanned by the scorching winds. The dried out ground and vegetation acted as instant fire fodder as the inferno mercilessly picked out houses and sheds in its pathway. The area was fortunately spared the loss of any lives.

IT ONLY TAKES THE SMALLEST THING TO MAKE THE BIGGEST THING

A house in Long Gully burns fiercely.

WE LOST EVERYTHING EXCEPT
OUR LIVES

I had just finished building my house in Redesdale last October and had finally moved in over December, after bringing my furniture down from Queensland where I had been living. My two children from Melbourne came up at Christmas for a family get together, which was like a house- warming.

The house was a renovated farm shed, which had been transformed into a very energy efficient, mud brick, two storey home. We used recycled power poles and bridge timbers, to support the mezzanine floor, and second hand corrugated iron and other materials, wherever possible. We had put in solar panels to supply all the power, as well as a system which recycled all the sewerage water, to irrigate the orchard. I had also installed a solar hot water system, and was very happy with my sustainable-energy building that achieved the level of comfort and self- sufficiency I had hoped for.

It was a long, hot summer, and I became concerned about the danger of bushfire, and began to plan how I could protect the house. The dam pump was being repaired, and underground pipes from the dam to the house had to be re-routed, and more hose connections to be installed around the house. I had contacted a plumber to assist with these jobs, and to install a sprinkler system on the house roof, but he was not available until February 9th.

THE HOT NORTH WIND FELT LIKE A BLAST FURNACE IN OUR FACES

Saturday 7th February arrived, and I got up early and cleared around the exterior of the house in preparation for the possible danger of fires. As predicted, it was an extremely hot day with temperatures reaching over 45°C. My son arrived for the weekend before lunch, and we kept inside most of the day as the house was cool. The hot north wind felt like a blast furnace in our faces when we ventured outside. It was amazing how cool the mud bricks kept the house.

At about twenty past three, my son Andrew, who was staying with me for a day, opened a window and said, "I can smell smoke, Mum!" We had heard no mention of any fires from the local Radio station, but I had just turned it off to answer the phone, and must have missed the announcement. Next thing, a neighbour to the east rang to say there was a fire nearby, but I assumed it to be in the south, and that it would be blown away from our place by the savage north westerly wind. My son then saw the fire coming over the hill to the north west, and at the same time I received a call from my daughter in Melbourne, saying they'd heard that there was a fire in our area and were wondering if we were all right. Little did we know of the ferocity of what lay ahead.

Andrew and I immediately put on fire protective clothing – long pants, goggles, face mask and gloves. I really started getting panicky now, but I knew there were a number of fire trucks in the neighbouring area and I thought that they would soon arrive and we would be OK. The fact was, we did not see a fire truck until it was all over. We watched in horror as fire and smoke started sweeping over the hill to the north of us, engulfing the house opposite. There was a mass of smoke, and you couldn't see exactly where the firefront was, but it seemed to pass just to the north of our property. The wind was wild and the embers started raining down everywhere.

I TRIED AND TRIED TO RING 000, BUT COULDN'T GET THROUGH

While Andrew was fighting spot fires caused by windblown embers, with a bucket and mop, I tried and tried and tried to ring 000, but couldn't get through. I assumed the CFA knew where the firefront was, because I had also received a phone call from a friend, whose husband had been called out on a fire truck. Finally the phone crackled and went dead; the line had obviously burnt through. We had very poor mobile phone coverage at the best of times, and it was a matter of luck to find a place on high ground, where there was some reception. At the height of the fire, we had no form of communication at all.

By this time we were frantic in our efforts, as the firestorm was raining embers on us with fires breaking out all around us. We then retreated back closer to the house, as the main fire spread from the roadside trees across the paddocks towards us. We were hosing and bucketing water on everything that was burning. When the water ran out, we started stamping out the flames, until the shed next to the house caught alight and began to burn fiercely. We had to retreat back inside the house to shelter from the radiant heat and the wild fire swirling around us. The wind and flames were now in a frenzy, and I checked upstairs in the house to make sure any burning embers were put out on the timber balcony facing the shed. I found one of the windows had cracked with the radiant heat from the now wildly burning shed.

Smoke smothers the town.

WE HAD TO SAVE OURSELVES OR IT WOULD BE TOO LATE

Looking south, we could see that the gully behind the house was now burning fiercely, and we were cut off from the dam. The water pump on the tank beside the house stopped working, and the fire surrounded three sides of the house. We still hoped we could save the house, but the embers had got past the mud bricks and started to catch alight the mezzanine floor. As we had no more water, I decided that was it; we must escape with our lives. We had to save ourselves, or it would be too late!

With no time to take anything, Andrew, Bessie the border collie and I raced to my vehicle, which fortunately was parked close to the back door. Andrew's car had to be left behind, which was incinerated. As I left I was confronted with an horrendous sight. Everything was in flames, from tiny herb plants to the water pump, the downpipes and all the plastic fittings. It was so hot, that whatever the fire touched, it burst into flames immediately, no matter how green or seemingly non-flammable it was.

To my relief the car motor started, and I was able to drive towards the front gate over ground that had been burnt in the first rush of flames, over grass which was short and sparse from the drought. Uncertain which direction to take, I drove away from the direction of the fire, avoiding burning trees along the roadside, and was able to get safely to my neighbours' house. His wife and children had already left, but the husband had stayed behind and managed to save the house. They had a good water supply, and sprinklers installed on the roof of the house. Andrew and I sheltered there, and helped put out spot fires for the next hour around the house. He was so grateful for our help, knowing we had just lost our own house. The burning trees were now falling across the road we had just come along, blocking the way out to Kyneton and Melbourne, where we could find beds for the night with family members.

THE AFTERMATH OF A BATTLE ZONE

Once the fire had started to settle down a little, we walked back over the burnt paddocks to my property, and viewed the burnt ruins of my dream home. I could not bear to look; it was such a scene of destruction. I was also very anxious to know if my neighbours to the north and east had survived, because they seemed to have been in the direct path of the firefront. The silent and desolate blackened land, now seemed like the aftermath of a battle zone. It was an awful sight of destruction that will be hard to erase from my mind. Dead birds, possums and animals lay around the ground, and our majestic trees were still burning and threatening to fall at any time. Nevertheless, we were overjoyed to realise that both neighbours and their houses had survived, and had safely evacuated with their children.

We decided to walk down to the highway to get some assistance and work out how we could get our car out of the neighbours' property. I tried to hail down at least five fire trucks as they drove past, but none of them stopped.

Eventually, some young men drove by in a car, and they generously offered to help us clear the side road so we could drive out onto the highway. They came back with a number of friends, and brought chainsaws to clear the burning trees, cutting and hauling the logs off the road, to clear a path so we could drive through. It was a risky job, as it was getting dark and more trees were falling all the time. They were so generous, cheerful and efficient, and put an end to our devastating sense of being alone in a catastrophe. It was hard to fully express our gratitude.

TREES WERE CRASHING DOWN AROUND US

The last obstacle looked impossible. A big tree at the front gate had been hollowed out by fire and was now burning like a giant candle and about to fall. Our helpers pushed the burning debris aside while I quickly dashed past in the car. We had to get out as fast as possible, as trees were crashing down all around us. I was also anxious to let my daughter know that we were OK. It was a huge relief to finally be able to drive to the safety of Kyneton.

It was a terrifying afternoon that I will never forget. The memories are unforgettably embedded in my mind. BLACK SATURDAY – a day that changed Victoria's history.

We were lucky, we lost everything but we escaped with our lives….JUST!!

Photo: HWT

SEARCHING FOR LOST TREASURES AMONGST THE RUBBLE.

CAROL REDDEN
Bendigo

Our home is one of the few houses in our area built around the turn of the century. William Ray was a mining magnate who operated a successful gold mine called Victorian Hill Goldmine across the road from our house. In the late 1800's he built a large heritage house with fluted concrete columns and ornate cornices decorating the beautifully constructed high ceiling home. This mansion was located on a large property directly behind our house. He also built our house for his son in 1900, and we have owned it since 1999.

On Saturday 7th of February, we first smelt smoke at about 3:30pm, and expected it to be just kids lighting fires in the gold mine property over the road, which was a regular occurrence. However there was no fire across the road. It appeared that the smoke was coming from miles away, so we climbed into the car and went for a drive to see where it was coming from. At the end of our street we could see the general direction of the fire, and by the time we drove back to our house 3 minutes later, fire was breaking out in the gold mine property just over the road!

Initially, I again thought this fire was lit by kids, so I told my son to go and ring 000, but he couldn't get through due to it being jammed by people ringing from all over Victoria where fires were raging, unbeknown to us. Looking back, it was obviously airborne sparks that caught the gold mine paddocks alight even though the main fire was still miles away.

CARS WERE EXPLODING AND GAS CYLINDERS WERE GOING OFF!

My neighbour from behind, who was renovating the old mansion, suggested we get all the hoses out and prepare the best we could. We ran up to the top of the hill and the fire still seemed miles away. Finally the fire started approaching us and we could see the flames and hear large bangs from cars exploding, and gas cylinders going off. The fire over the road was blowing away from our house, so I still wasn't overly concerned. The neighbour decided he would get his wife and kids to safety and told me he was leaving.

100 YEARS OF HERITAGE
DESTROYED

The history of this heritage home lies beneath its charred exterior.

It was about 5:00pm and I told one of my twin sons to grab the hose and keep guard out the back watching for any ember attack that would cause fire spotting around the house.

Suddenly, a lot of airborne embers started attacking the property. It was like a huge fireworks display with showers of sparks and the radiant heat was intense. My son in desperation called out to me, "Mum, it's not working, there's too many fires."

I called back, "Just stand there and put the fires out," but realised only a minute later it was far too much to handle. The embers were severe and just took over the bush at the back of the property. The neighbour's old horse stables were now burning fiercely and this increased the intensity of the fire which was still blowing away from our house, giving me a false sense of security.

Two firemen drove past in a vehicle and I hailed them down to come and help. The two of them said, "Listen, you'll have to leave and get out of the area."

I said; "I can't, it's all I possess and I want to protect it." They were insistent that we leave.

After expressing my desire to stay, my son actually picked me up and said, "We're going Mum".

The other two kids were still inside, and unbeknown to me, my daughter had packed the baby photo album into the car, and my son had packed his soccer ball, football and rugby ball in as well. With great resistance, I was finally coerced to leave the house by firemen and kids alike, so I grabbed my bag and we got into the car and onto the road. We were amazed to find the road choked, bumper to bumper with sightseers' vehicles slowing our escape from the danger. We finally arrived at my parents' home in the Golden Triangle three kilometre away, at about 5:45pm. I still wasn't overly concerned that I would lose the house, and kept remarkably calm.

JETS OF FIRE 2-3 METRES HIGH

At about 7:45pm, I tried to drive back to our house with the kids, but the streets were blocked. Finally, I was able to drive up the street behind our house. There were houses burning everywhere and broken gas lines were whooshing up jets of fire 2-3 metres high into the air.

It was only when we ran over some fallen power lines that the kids yelled to me; "Get out Mum, let's get the hell out of here, we've just driven over some power lines!" I still couldn't tell if our house had survived or not.

Then came that devastating call at 10:30pm that evening. A friend phoned to confirm that our house was burning from the inside. We returned at last to find the walls still standing, but it was too late. The grand old house had been completely gutted.

I remember with horror the broken dreams and blackened memories that surround that terrible day for me and several of my loved neighbours. We will rebuild our house with the same bricks, which we are cleaning ourselves to save cost. At least we still have each other.

0.1 FENCE FLATTENED.

0.2 MASS DESTRUCTION.

0.3 HOME FOR SALE?

0.4 HOUSE ERADICATED.

0.5 LONELY SHELL.

0.6 AN ANTENNA SENTINEL.

0.7 AWAITING CLEANUP.

0.8 CHIMNEYS, LIKE HEAD STONES.

THERE WERE HOUSES BURNING EVERYWHERE

0.1

0.1 Bendigo City under threat.
0.2 Fire rips through another Bendigo home.

0.2

HIGH COUNTRY
ERUPTS

BEECHWORTH IS ONE OF VICTORIA'S OLDEST TOWNS NESTLED IN THE HIGH COUNTRY ON THE RIDGE OF THE GREAT DIVIDING RANGE. THIS TOWNSHIP, SURROUNDED BY ORCHARDS AND VINEYARDS, IS A POPULAR TOURIST LOCATION KNOWN FOR ITS GLOWING COLOURS THAT ARE SO PROMINENT DURING EARLY AUTUMN.

Photo: HWT

0.1 A LOCAL RESIDENT ASSISTS FIREFIGHTING CREWS PLAN FOR BATTLE.

0.2 A MIRACULOUS OUTCOME AGAINST A STARK LANDSCAPE.

Photo: HWT

0.3 A STRAINED AND WEARY FIREMAN CLEARS SOOT FROM HIS EYE.

0.4 RESIDENT WIELDS A GARDEN HOSE IN A VAIN ATTEMPT TO EXTINGUISH THE MERCILESS FIRE.

BEECHWORTH
MUDGEGONGA

BEECHWORTH

Beechworth Wangaratta Rd

MELBOURNE 216KM

MUDGEGONGA

DATING BACK TO THE GOLD RUSH DAYS WHEN THE TOWN BUSTLED WITH MEN AND WOMEN WHO HAD COME TO MAKE THEIR FORTUNE, IT ALWAYS CARRIED THE CHARACTER OF A BOOMING GOLD TOWN. THE TOWN CAN BOAST HOLDING SOME OF AUSTRALIA'S MOST NOTORIOUS CRIMINALS AND BUSHRANGERS IN ITS OLD SAND-STONE JAIL HOUSE WHILST THE COURT HOUSE GAVE MANY A FAREWELL TO SUCH BUSHRANGERS WHO WERE DESTINED FOR MELBOURNE'S GALLOWS.

Beechworth and Mudgegonga are both surrounded by towering mountain ashes and snow gum trees, both belonging to the eucalypt species, which emit an explosive vapour in extreme heat. With deep wooded gullies and steep sweeping hills dotted with farms in between the forested swaths of mountainous areas, it has always been a place where fires have been feared. Over the years these mountain towns have been threatened regularly by raging fires, but nothing compared even remotely to the terror of Black Saturday.

It would appear that the fires started by trees falling onto power lines, just three kilometres south of Beechworth, near Buckland Gap Road. With the violent winds behind the flames, it soon was fanned into an all engulfing blanket of fire that grew faster than even the most experienced firefighters had ever witnessed before.

The fire then ripped through Mudgegonga and other nearby areas, a pastoral and close knit social community, which is south east of Beechworth. As one resident said, "It simply flattened everything in its path." The fire consumed an estimated 30,000 ha of state forests and private properties, with farmers losing stock totaling into the hundreds.

Into the night the fire swept down the valleys through plantations and over the ridges. Over the next few days the emergency services were forced in a last ditch effort to throw everything at the fires to contain them, often fighting in almost inaccessible areas because of the steep and densely wooded terrain.

Finally it was brought under control, but not before the loss of two lives and twenty nine dwellings.

The people of this beautiful district in the highlands of Northern Victoria will continue to work together to mend and rebuild as a result of the damage caused by Australia's worst natural disaster.

Photo: HWT

EVERYTHING IN ITS PATH

Photo: Associated Press

Photo: Newspix

Photo: Newspix

HER HAIR
WAS ON FIRE

Captain Barry Mapley, of the Eurobin firetruck, had been told to attend the fire on the outskirts of Beechworth at about 6:40pm on the evening of 7th February. Barry's son had already left with a strike team earlier in the afternoon, to attend the fires near Kinglake, and now the only trucks left in the area were called to action at Beechworth, about twenty kilometres away.

Barry recalls getting to Mudgegonga with his crew, consisting of Mark Bursill, Terry Lockwood and Shaun Raoss.

We could see the glow of the fire above the forest and as I got nearer, the roar of the fire got louder and louder. About 15-20 minutes after we arrived, the fire started breaking out with ember attack as it forced its way through the forest.

IT WAS LIKE HELL ON EARTH!

This fire was far worse than anything we had witnessed in the earlier 1983 and 2003 fires and I'm sure we would have lost many more townships nearby if this fire had started earlier in the afternoon. It was like hell on Earth, but at least we had some relief from the intensity of the sun with the hot wind, due to nightfall approaching.

A MAYDAY distress signal then came over the radio, calling for urgent help. Rosewhite Tanker was fighting the fires two kilometres away on a nearby property and had a burn-over (The fire overran the firetruck). We raced to their assistance along Switchback Rd. We located the property and were getting closer to where we knew they would be, when they called us off saying they had just got clear and were now OK.

"A VERY NEAR CALL."

Suddenly, as we passed a farm house on the property the fire caught the house alight. We pulled alongside to try and save the house, and after putting out the fire on one side of the house, we realised the other side of the house had caught alight under the verandah.

Glowing airborne embers were hurtling through the air. Everywhere you looked was under flame-attack, and it was horrific to witness the deafening roar of the fire that was swirling around us. We stayed on the truck for some protection as we pulled around the other side of the house. As we started hosing the verandah, a shed nearby burst into flames, and the gap between the house and the shed then erupted in a tunnel of wild fire.

A BBQ GAS BOTTLE ON THE BACK VERANDAH THEN BLEW UP!

A BBQ gas bottle on the back verandah then blew up and ripped the verandah roof off the back of the house in the explosion. Fire was all around us and underneath the truck. It was full on! Mark then noticed a large gas bottle further along the verandah, and yelled - "Let's get out of here, we're going to

die!" I made the decision to go, and reversed out of there as fast as I could to save our skins.

As we got clear of the house, the ute driven by Paul Mercieca came tearing towards us. Mark yelled again STOP! I slammed on the brakes not knowing what I was reversing into as Paul pulled alongside the truck and yelled out, "Where can I go, will I make a run for it?"

Mark yelled back over the roar of the flames, "No, stay right there!" He immediately trained the fire hose on the back of the ute where flames were leaping from an LP gas tank. Beside the gas tank was Paul's girl friend Amelia Coombes, who was frantically holding onto her two dogs. Her hair had caught fire from the burning gas tank, and staring death in the face, she had stayed on the ute, hoping the flashing lights of the firetruck might bring safety. Mark and Shaun doused the flames with fire hoses, and with help of a fire blanket, the gas bottle flames and Amelia's hair were extinguished. For the next five to ten minutes, Mark and Shaun created a fog of water over the two vehicles, in a desperate bid to save them all from being enveloped in fire.

The flames were traveling at about eighty kilometres per hour and there was absolutely nowhere to go.

Paul had two more dogs in the cab of the ute, along with two pet python snakes. The two of them and animals alike, were right beside death's door prior to pulling alongside the firetruck. Paul had driven round and round the paddock trying to escape the fire which was burning wildly everywhere he looked. He saw the firetruck none too soon and rushed over to us for assistance.

THE FIRE WENT UNDER US AND OVER THEM!

We shielded them whilst we too hung it out. The fire went under us and over them, howling, spitting and growling in a frenzy of flames.

We finally got out of there and continued fighting the fires through the night, before stopping at about 6:00am the next morning. We witnessed houses burning to the ground, but saved many as well, with trip after trip to fill up at water points. What an unstoppable fire. I'm just thankful to be alive after that night of horror.

I can still remember a house with skylights, and the embers had burnt through the top of the skylights. In no time it was like a chimney with fire and smoke pouring through the roof, as the fire burnt from inside out.

"I'm not a hero, it's the Australian way, but we saved them- no doubt." said Gary later. 'They'd have been toasted if they made a run for it.' Paul and Amelia shed tears as they recalled their experience with Barry the next day.

EVERYWHERE YOU LOOKED WAS UNDER FLAME-ATTACK.

FIRE
CYCLONE

HORSHAM IS A THRIVING CITY LOCATED ON THE WIMMERA RIVER IN THE CENTRAL WEST OF VICTORIA AND HAS GROWN STEADILY OVER THE LAST 150 YEARS ON THE BACK OF A FLOURISHING SHEEP AND FARMING INDUSTRY.

Photo: HWT

0.1 THE CHARRED SKELETON OF HORSHAM GOLF CLUB

0.2 HORSHAM GOLFERS BACK ON THE COURSE.

0.3 A FIREMAN CUTS A LONELY SILHOUETTE AGAINST THE EERIE GLOW.

0.4 TREES STAND DEFIANT AGAINST AN ERUPTION OF FIRE.

HORSHAM
COLERAINE

HORSHAM

MELBOURNE 275KM

Henty Hwy

Stawell

COLERAINE

Hamilton

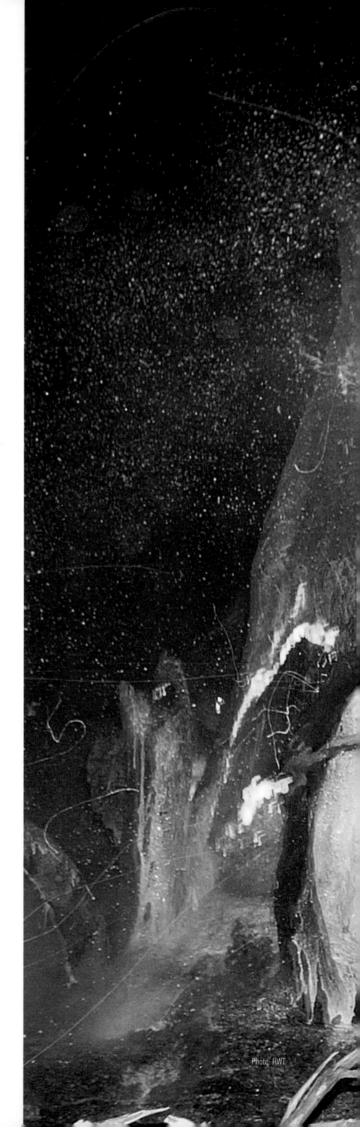

HORSHAM

Its location on the main Western Hwy between Melbourne and Adelaide has also benefited the local trade with tourists attracted by nearby wineries and the renowned Grampians, a rugged mountain range with picturesque waterfalls and precarious rock faces all interwoven with popular bushwalks. The closest major inland cities include Ballarat to the east and Hamilton to the south.

Saturday was an extremely hot and windy day, but this of course is very common for an inland city, and being in the midst of farmland, bushfires have never been any great threat.

Black Saturday was to be an entirely different scenario for Horsham, as the residents quickly found out to their horror! In such ferocious winds it appears that power lines may have been blown from their poles on to the tinder dry grasslands surrounding Horsham. At 12:26pm the first fire was reported, and the local CFA threw everything at it to contain the fire before it spread towards the city.

The fire took off like a cyclone across the grasslands, devouring everything in its path, showing no mercy to animal or property. It then quickly spread into an area of wooded bushland where it gathered strength and intensity before bursting from the trees, "roaring and exploding" as one resident described it! After descending onto the local Horsham golf course, the fire headed rapidly for the city. In its destructive swath, it consumed the well known golf house before moving on to claim 68 residential homes. Mercifully, no lives were lost but many came close to succumbing to the fire's awesome strength.

Wind changes took the blaze on a horseshoe-shaped route around the edge of the town before firefighters finally extinguished the flames at 6:30pm on the edge of a large goat farm, east of Horsham.

It burnt a total of 2,200 hectares of land, 68 homes, many farm sheds and countless animals and wildlife.

COLERAINE

Coleraine is a farming community of approximately 2000 residents in Western Victoria, 31 kilometres from Hamilton. It is an old township and not unlike Horsham, has survived on sheep farming since early days.

Black Saturday's fire started in the nearby hills on farming property. It spread rapidly and quickly jumped main roads heading straight for the town. The fire burnt to the edge of the town, taking with it 775 hectares of prime farm land.

The Premier of Victoria, John Brumby, has parents living in Coleraine, and the fire burnt right to the edge of their property on the outskirts of the town. Mr. Brumby appeared visibly upset on a TV program, as he described the way the fires were heading towards his parents' home, and how seemingly helpless he was to assist them.

The wind change finally helped the CFA contain the fire there at 5:30pm on Black Saturday.

Photo: HWT

0.1 THE MOLTEN REMAINS OF THE INTERIOR OF THIS VEHICLE SHOWCASE THE FIRE'S SEVERITY.

0.2 THE SMOLDERING REMAINS OF THE HORSHAM CLUB HOUSE ARE DOUSED WITH WATER.

0.3 BLACK SATURDAY'S CARNAGE IS LEFT TO FIRE CREWS TO UNRAVEL.

0.4 ANOTHER CAR THAT SUCCUMBED TO THE FURY OF THE FIRESTORM.

THE FIRE TOOK OFF LIKE A CYCLONE ACROSS THE GRASS LANDS

BRAXTON SAVES
HIS WOOLLY FRIENDS

TED BROWN
Horsham

Horsham residents were shaken after realizing how much worse the fires could have been on Saturday 7th February. Even so, the fire burnt about 2300 hectares, sixty eight homes, the Golf Club, a CFA vehicle, many sheds and cars, and a huge quantity of farm fencing.

The fire originally started at Renshaw, but within minutes it had grown to a 1.5 kilometre front, jumping over Natimuk Road and the Wimmera River, just missing a housing estate at the edge of Horsham.

The fire then swept over to Horsham Golf Club where large trees caught alight and engulfed the club house as it raced around the edge of the town. The fire then came across the Henty Hwy, then across the back of properties along Hunts Road, where my property was located.

I had left to drive up to Adelaide, where I was going to catch a plane to Broome to see my daughters. When my mate Simon Stevenson heard on the radio that the fire was in the Haven area, he drove round to see what he could do as he knew that I was on my way to Broome. It took him quite a while to get there as he had to dodge the roadblocks, but he finally got through to my place about 12:30pm, where he stayed until about 8:00pm. I turned around at Keith and got back to Horsham about 5:30, but I couldn't get past the roadblock until about 11:00pm that night. When I finally got back home I was able to watch over the house all night.

Simon and Alex (my next door neighbour) were just standing there, on the back of my property looking out across the paddocks as the fire raced towards a house between the trees. One second the house was there and the next it wasn't – just boom! It was gone; it exploded into flames and disappeared. All that was left were two brick chimneys and a pile of burning rubble, it just blew up and disintegrated.

As for the pine trees – there are only about a quarter of them left intact compared with what there used to be. There was a long line of pine trees at the back of my neighbour's place and they just went boom, boom, boom, and the whole lot was burnt. They just exploded as the fire hit them. The gum trees were even worse – just one almighty boom and they were all ablaze. The boys thought it was paint tins exploding at the primary school, which was over on the highway, but it wasn't, it was the vapour of the gum trees exploding.

The noise was like fireworks, like crackers going off beside you. My friend Clark lost his B double tipper – didn't lose the prime mover, just the trailers.

It took Simon a fair effort to save my shed. There was another little shed tacked on the side of it and Simon saw the smoke coming out of it when he opened the door and yelled to the fire brigade, "Fill it! Full of water!"

Then the nearby container went up- a twenty foot container full of antiques. Man, I could have cried!

They were helping each other – Simon and Alex (my next door neighbour). They would keep checking on each other – both had their own fires to fight, but Simon would go over to him to see if he was going all right and Alex would come over to our place to check on Simon.

The fire got into Doug's house over the road through the air conditioner on the roof. The fire went down the ducts of his house and did a fair bit of damage. The firey's actually got on the roof and hosed water through the air conditioner. The damage in the house was mainly because of the water.

The firemen said to Simon when they first arrived, "Have you got Doug's number?" He had the work mobile, so he called him and got his message bank which said, "You've called Dougo, I'm either out loading my truck, tying down, having a sleep, having a beer or playing golf!" He didn't get onto him till 6:00pm because he was in fact playing golf down at Portland all day whilst his house was burning back at home.

The neighbour's alpaca, called Braxton, did an amazing job looking after my sheep when the fires hit us. The alpaca took them up the fence line against the road whilst the fire was going through and held them there for a couple of hours, then sometime during the night they wandered off across the blackened paddocks. Braxton went with them for protection because dogs just hunt the sheep, and foxes are really bad news too! The alpaca protected the sheep down in the area that was already burnt. Braxton has a bond with my sheep and fiercely protects his woolly friends and he took them away from the smoke. The next day a search finally discovered the buddies 1.5 kilometre away, and as they were heading across the paddocks, they heard my familiar whistle and Braxton marched them right on home. There is no way we could separate Braxton from the sheep, he is like a guardian angel and won't part company with them.

The fire came through here incredibly fast a second time and my nephew said the fire was hurtling through the air about ten feet off the ground, it wasn't burning anything, just pure flame. The heat and smoke were massively intense as well – Simon and Alex suffered a little from asphyxiation, as they couldn't leave the fire long enough to go and get a drink of water. Simon finally got a couple of beers at about 7:30 that night!

We had a million dollars worth of machinery here, a twenty five tonne mobile crane, a twenty five tonne excavator, an eight tonne excavator, a big Komatsu four wheel drive loader, a smaller excavator and a bobcat. We didn't lose any of it, Simon saved all of it. We were incredibly fortunate and I can't thank everyone enough. Simon really saved a lot of property and I am very grateful.

The firey's also did a great job on the day!

Photo: HWT

An exploding tree provides a startling display of fireworks.

FERN GULLIES AND WILDLIFE
THREATENED

FERNTREE GULLY AND UPWEY FORM PART OF THE GATEWAY TO THE DANDENONG RANGES WHICH ARE RENOWNED FOR BEAUTIFUL FERN GULLIES, TALL MOUNTAIN GUMS AND ABUNDANT WILDLIFE SUCH AS WALLABIES, WEDGE-TAIL EAGLES, KOOKABURRAS, KOALAS AND LYREBIRDS.

If you were to walk quietly on a misty morning into Sherbrooke Forest or some of the other lush green forest areas that dominate these ranges, it would not be uncommon to hear a multitude of bird noises floating through the still crisp air. The fires of Upwey and Upper Ferntree Gully were literally on the door step of this majestic mountain range, as firefighters held them back with fire trucks and water dumping helicopters. The fires threatened to wipe out townships tucked into the foothills, and it was only the brave and tireless efforts of the firefighters that stopped these fires from destroying more lives and homes than they did. Black Saturday brought a fire outbreak on the edge of an old quarry in the Ferntree Gully area. This fire spread rapidly and threatened to escalate into a monster but for the CFA's prompt reaction. The western face of the Dandenong Ranges is one of the worst fire prone areas in the world and houses thousands of families who rely heavily of the CFA to keep them safe each summer. This fire was contained immediately, but within a week there was to be others that would threaten the communities that populate these areas.

Thanks once again to the tireless effort of the emergency services, there was no loss of life and the locals could breath again safely until next fire season.

NARRE WARREN

This nearby hobby farm district, surrounded by beautiful homes alongside the leafy Berwick township, is a greenscape that opens the door to Gippsland. This fire could have wreaked havoc throughout the region had it not been checked by the prompt and courageous efforts of the CFA.

Photo: HWT

0.1 A STRIKE TEAM PREPARES FOR ACTION

0.2 FIREMEN DOUSE THE REMAINING EMBERS AT A DISUSED QUARRY IN UPPER FERNTREE GULLY.

0.3 A SINGED KANGAROO BOUNDS TO SAFER TERRITORY. LUCKY TO HAVE SURVIVED.

0.4 A BEAUTIFUL HOME IS THREATENED BY A HUGE FRONT OF FIRE.

UPPER FERNTREE GULLY, UPWEY
NARRE WARREN NORTH

UPPER FERNTREE GULLY

Burwood Hwy

UPWEY

MELBOURNE 31KM

NARRE WARREN NORTH

PETER SMITH

Upper Ferntree Gully

Upper Ferntree Gully CFA Station is based right at the foot of the Dandenong mountains on the east side of Melbourne and we have two big tanker trucks and a "slip on" ute, which is a dual cab Land Rover with a removable water tank and pump unit. We had fought a couple of fires in January, including quite a nasty one in Churchill National Park. I had four of my junior firemen end up in hospital from dehydration that day on Friday 30th January. We thought that was bad, but worse was still to come.

Conditions had been consistently extreme through late January and early February, and by the time we got to Black Saturday 7th February, we were on high alert with demand for our trucks spread over several areas. The method of operations in the CFA is to go where the fires are, not just wait in case a fire comes to you. We have had many days over 40°C when there was no fire anywhere near us. On Saturday 7th February, we sent our first truck down to Bunyip Ridge, some 60 kilometres away, to fight the fires there at 10:30am, then later in the afternoon I took a truck up behind the station to Quarry Road to join some other trucks fighting a fire there. There were about twelve CFA tanker trucks there finally, fighting the fire around the quarry and the railway line. A helicopter (with a 2000 litre tank underneath) spent 15 minutes helping us try to contain it. Not one house was lost, just a car! Later in the day we also helped fight a fire in Narre Warren that is reported to have started from a man using an angle grinder near long grass. The two trucks didn't get back till Sunday morning.

On Sunday 8th February we sent one truck to help out at Wallan, and another to Kinglake, where major fires were burning. One of those trucks stayed up there for about ten days or more. On Tuesday 10th February we were called to a house fire in the early hours of the morning that belonged to one of our crew at the station. He died in the house and it was almost too much for us by the time we had the funeral later that week. As he had been a valuable member of our team, it really took its toll.

By Tuesday 23rd February I actually decided to return to work at my day job. My boss said, "What are you doing here?" He must have thought I was needed on duty as a CFA Captain. I went back home and then returned to the station. It was about 2:30pm when my 1st lieutenant, Michael, called past the station and shared his feelings with me. We felt tense and on edge and we both said it was eerie, but we couldn't explain why. The wind was high and the temperature was soaring. It was a really volatile day. Then my 3rd

lieutenant, Mark, drove up and stopped. I asked him what he was doing and he said, "I guess the same as you two." We had a bit of a talk out the front at about 2:45pm and while we were talking we noticed a column of smoke in the south east. Next thing we heard Upwey fire alarm going off in the distance, so we went inside to listen to the CFA radio. There was a fire at Bird's Paddock, Nixon's Lane in Lysterfield. I said, "Let's get dressed." While we were pulling on our boots, our pagers went, and then the siren went off automatically on our station tower.

Adrenalin was starting to kick in, but we decided to wait for a couple of minutes for our other two men on call in the area. After waiting a couple of minutes we decided that we'd have to go. We were three very experienced firemen, so we set off towards Bird's Paddock, off Wellington Road.

WE STILL COULDN'T SEE THE FIRE
After hearing on the two-way radio that a Ferntree Gully truck needed a bit of help on one of the tracks, and knowing that the Scoresby truck was still about four minutes away, we drove up to a house situated right on the edge of the heavy bush and waited for the Scoresby truck. We still couldn't see the fire, but from radio reports it was heading towards us.

The Scoresby truck turned up and we decided together to head up the fire track to try and knock the head off the fire. The grass was only about 30cm high and conditions were reasonably calm, so we felt that the best solution was to try and catch the fire before it jumped over the track.

We got going and went to work. Rolling out two hoses as the fire approached us, it was going fairly well, with the fire behaving reasonably normally, all things considered. The head of the fire was now being pincered with our fire plan and the 1.5m high flames were gradually being brought under control. In the main, the flames were only burning the undergrowth and grass and not getting into the crown of the trees. However, we noticed a slight wind change had occurred. Radio contact had been lost with the thick smoke knocking out the transmission. Now we only had contact between trucks nearby; no contact with CFA command. The wind changed four times over the next 15 minutes and everything started really going up. One minute the flames were 1.5m high with hardly any wind, and embers were being thrown only about 10m to 15m in front of the fire, next minute or two the flames became 3.5m high, with the intensity of the fire really turning ugly. We realised the wind had changed, with embers starting to spot much further ahead, going right over the truck into the unburnt area. Mick was on the truck operating the pump, so he rolled another hose out and began putting out spot fires on the other side of the truck. Then the fire really got a grip over us. We looked at each other and we all knew what we were thinking. That's it! We had to get out of there! The flank of the fire had turned into the head, and was rapidly bearing down on us! It was really going wild!

IT WAS SO HOT, THE WATER WAS EVAPORATING BEFORE IT GOT TO THE FLAMES!
We started moving backwards towards the fire truck, still holding the hoses at the firefront which was accelerating towards us. The main fire was only about two to three metres away and our water wasn't even touching the

FIRE CAPTAIN

WE THOUGHT IT WAS BAD BUT WORSE WAS STILL TO COME.

fire. It was so hot, the water was evaporating before it got to the flames! By the time we got to the truck, there were flames all around us. Mick had launched himself into the driver's seat and Mark got into the back of the dual cab. Lastly I got in into the front passenger seat after making sure we were all safe in the truck. We then tried to yell to the Scoresby truck to get a couple of their fellows into our more modern truck. They had an older style truck with a single cab, and three blokes were in the back of the truck with fire blankets over them. As they drove off, the diesel line to their truck's fire pump at the rear actually burnt through, spraying diesel over the back of the truck, causing it to catch on fire, and a hole burning right through the rear end of the truck. It's one reason fire trucks only use diesel engines, as it's not explosive like petrol.

"GET THE CURTAINS DOWN!"

They got going and we watched them driving through the flames away from us. By this time the firefront was engulfing our truck. The flames were well and truly higher than the roof of the truck. I said to Mick, "What's the chance?"

He replied, "I can't see a thing out the front or the back."

So I said, "Get the curtains down!" We dropped all the fireproof curtains inside the windows. These completely block off all the windows including the windscreen. Even though we were experienced fire fighters, it was fairly hair-raising. We activated the sprinklers around the roof of the truck and hung on. Mark commented at one time, "Far out, it's getting hot."

I yelled back at him to "Shut up, because it's hotter outside! Just do what we are doing, because it's right!" The fire was at screaming point by this stage, and the truck was rocking with the wind. We could hear the crackling of the fire against the metal of the cab, relentless in its hellfire fury. We had trained for this type of event many times and we were remarkably calm.

THE FLAMES THEN LEAPT THROUGH THE GAP AND LIT UP THE DASHBOARD

Through the roar of the fire hammering the cabin, the passenger cab window broke, and shattered in an exploding crack. Moments later Mick's driver side window also disintegrated in the inferno. His curtains held shut with the Velcro straps, but mine gave way as the blaze blistered the Velcro where the front curtain joined the side curtain. The flames then leapt through the gap and lit up the dashboard. It was full on. Whilst we were hanging on to our lives, the fire was testing every weak point of our barrier. I put out the flames on the dashboard with my feet, whilst holding the curtain shut with my hands.

At this stage I yelled to Mick over the roar of the fire to try reversing. I had remembered the track was fairly straight just prior to stopping, so Mick started reversing back. We couldn't see a thing with the curtains down. Mick actually pulled his curtain back a bit to look in the mirror, only to find the rubber seals around the door mirror on fire, and the mirror shattered. He quickly shut the curtain over the flames to stop them entering the cabin. We reversed backwards about 50m until we hit a tree. I yelled to Mick to try again, so he pulled forward and tried reversing again. We got about another 30m before hitting a big tree and then the truck just died. It was the end of the line for our truck. Would we get out or wait?

The cab had been filling up with acrid smoke from the burning dashboard

We were now struggling with our breathing. Time was running out. I asked Mark, "How's it going? Is your Velcro holding?"

"Yep," he replied. We tried numerous times to get 'Maydays' out, but it was to no avail as radio contact was nil. I could hear the Scoresby truck calling us on my portable radio that I had shoved down the front of my shirt. I knew they were in the thick of it too, but had hoped they had got into a clearing, which is exactly what they were able to do, as we found out later. I asked Mark to check what the driver's side of the truck was like, so he pulled the curtain back, checked it out and said, "It's looking a bit easier." The main firefront seemed to have passed, and the secondary fire – a lower intensity, ember driven fire that was burning the trees and the bushy crown of the trees, was now all around us. We knew we had to try and get out.

The passenger side of the truck was alight, and well and truly burning, so it was the driver's side or not at all. Mark and Mick both got out with the big red woollen blankets, and I threw them the two water bottles from the centre console. Being a reasonably big guy, I was struggling to get over the centre console and out. It was going to be a massive task. Every time I let the curtains go, the fire thrust into the cabin again. Mick, being 6'2" and strong, yelled to me to hold his arms so he could drag me out. Using my foot to keep the curtains shut I removed my helmet, and held it in my left hand so I wouldn't knock Mick out. With every muscle in my body poised, I shot out that doorway faster than a cat on hot bricks and hit my chest on Mick's shoulder before landing on my feet next to him. We started to laugh. Mark asked what we were laughing about, and Mick exclaimed, "Mud Guts (my nickname) has landed on his feet!"

I said, "We're not discussing such trivial things now because we just have to get to safety!" Don't ask me how we did it, but it's amazing what you can do in extreme circumstances. Just as we got clear of the truck, we saw the inside of the cabin explode into flames.

WE WOULD HAVE BEEN FRIED IF WE'D STAYED IN THERE ANY LONGER

Fully exposed now to the surrounding fire, we threw the two blankets over us all and waddled in a threesome up the track to a bit of a clearing. Never could we have survived without those blankets. They saved our bacon. Locating the main track, we got back to the house we had started from about 500 metres away. The fire was heading towards the house, and climbing aboard another fire truck, we helped the crew save this house. Earlier, we had got messages through to the Scoresby truck to tell them "We're out." The Scoresby truck then turned up at the house, a little singed but with all the crew members OK. Two Skycrane helicopters flew in and dropped four loads of water – nine tons each load, directly around the house. What a miracle – another victory!

We climbed aboard the Scoresby truck and retreated to the safety of the main road nearby. Ambulance, police and fire crews were anxiously waiting for us on Wellington Road.

By this stage we realised that it had been reported on CFA radio that a truck had burnt out and two crew had perished, and one critically injured. Due to lack of radio contact, this had been the expected outcome, but we were incredibly relieved to ring our wives and break the news that we were all OK. After all, a $350,000 truck cannot compare with the cost of human lives. It was an amazing situation caused by the unpredictable firefront due to wind changes.

Someone was smiling on me that day. Despite the CFA life-saving training that had worked to perfection, I was aware that Someone up top was my preserver, and I'm not a churchy person. The most religious thing I've ever done is barrack for St Kilda football team..... "Go the mighty Saints!"

0.1 Elvis swoops in for another water drop.

0.2 Just in time as flames threaten...

0.3 Residents flee as water descends...
0.4 The precision drop smothers the flames- Elvis saves the day!

0.3

0.4

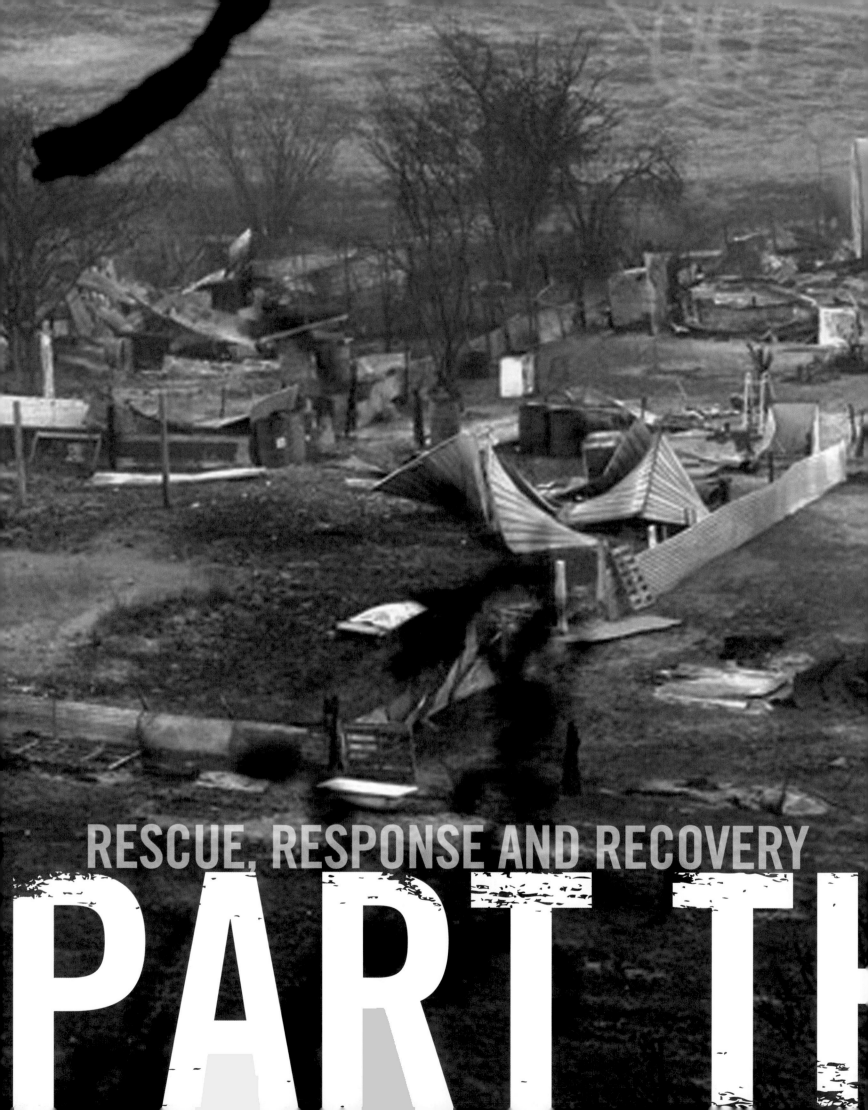

RESCUE, RESPONSE AND RECOVERY
PART TH

0.1 A COMMUNITY MEETING AT MARYSVILLE AFTER THE FIRES, BOOSTING THE MORALE OF THE TOWNSFOLK.

0.2 LIFE MUST GO ON FOR MANY WHO LOST THEIR HOMES. TEMPORARY HOUSES ARE ERECTED FOR THE HOMELESS

0.3 THE BEGINNING OF A NEW LIFE. HOUSES ARE REBUILT.

0.4 THE GUM TREE HAS AN AMAZING WAY OF REPAIRING ITSELF

VICTORIAN BUSHFIRE RECONSTRUCTION AND RECOVERY AUTHORITY

CHRISTINE NIXON had already announced her retirement as Victoria Police Chief Commissioner, when she was chosen to head the new Bushfire Reconstruction Authority.

Standing together, silent, surrounded by an array of ash and debris in Marysville, Premier John Brumby turned to then Victoria Police Chief Commissioner Christine Nixon and posed a question. Would she consider heading up the Victorian Bushfire Reconstruction and Recovery Authority, to help rebuild Marysville and the other fire affected communities?

Ms Nixon acknowledged the road to recovery would not be easy, but it was one she was committed to, as were the issues it invoked.

"Amongst the disaster, I heard countless stories of heartbreak and hope. I saw an incredible determination to rebound and rebuild and it was important to communicate that."

"We will be working with the Royal Commission about what type of houses should be rebuilt. Our Authority will then be in a position to give residents and local councils advice."

"I think the other issue for people to consider is whether to stay and prepare, or to go, in an event of another bushfire. I think that is an early lesson people will have to consider for the future"

EMERGENCY ACCOMMODATION

The first stage of the recovery program was to provide emergency accommodation, which was done for over 7000 homeless victims at relief centres. Whole townships and entire communities had vanished overnight which strained resources to breaking point, yet an amazing outpouring of sympathy combined with an unparalled spirit of giving have contributed to people getting back on their feet again. Government departments, Red Cross and other agencies combined to help relocate the townsfolk who had been left homeless into temporary housing constructed on open paddocks. Small townships of temporary homes sprang up near where the towns had once stood in each of the affected areas.

REBUILDING

The Building Commission has written new regulations for houses being built in fire areas, which will increase the resilient character of the house to withstand bushfires in the future. Several Bushfire Attack Levels (B.A.L's.) have also been determined, resulting from varying degrees of danger created by surrounding vegetation.

Many people have started rebuilding already beside the blackened backdrops that surround their properties.

0.5 FRESH GROWTH AMID DESTRUCTION

0.6 FERNS ARE ONE OF THE FIRST TO REGROW AFTER INTENSE HEAT. SIGNS LIKE THIS MAKE IT LOOK PROMISING

0.7 THE 'CLEAN UP' OPERATION BEGINS. IT TOOK HUNDREDS OF TRUCK LOADS TO CLEAR THE CARNAGE

0.8 REBUILDING OUR HOMES, REBUILDING OUR LIVES.

GOVERNMENT
SYMPATHY

The Prime Minister, Kevin Rudd, toured many of the fire affected areas during the week after the bushfires. He met many fire victims and fire crews who bravely fought the horror fires of Black Saturday, and viewed the distressing aftermath of areas that had once been beautiful country havens.

He praised the legion of heroes who had done everything humanly possible to prevent even more deaths."February 7th 2009, will become etched into our national memory as a day of death, disaster and mourning," Mr Rudd told a Parliament sitting that was marked by an eerie silence during the condolence motion. The Governor – General, Quentin Bryce has requested a national effort of the greatest generosity of spirit to help bushfire victims.

Mr. Russell Broadbent, a Victorian MP, was applauded after making a moving speech to the Parliament. "I know there are people who will wake every morning believing that it was all a dream, that it did not happen", he said. "And then they will realise it was not a dream and they will cry and they will cry again." Mr. Broadbent, a volunteer firefighter himself, stunned MP's as he choked with emotion and feelings when describing the 'awesome fury' of an approaching fire.

"Coming out of the Bunyip State Forest just before it broke into open ground, the fire ripped out a 200 foot high mountain ash gum tree, threw it into the air and dropped it on the ground as if it were a twig," he said. Such was the velocity and force of the wind, combined with the oppressive heat. It came as an onslaught against property owners and firemen alike.

The Nation was struck by extensive flood damage in Northern Queensland, whilst at the same time, nature's fury unleashed its devastation with the fires through Victoria in the south. The Prime Minister received an extraordinary number of calls of support and offers of help from overseas government leaders including US President Barack Obama.

QUEEN'S MESSAGE

HER MAJESTY, QUEEN ELIZABETH II, SENT A MESSAGE OF CONDOLENCE TO THE VICTIMS, EMERGENCY SERVICES AND ALL AUSTRALIANS IN RELATION TO THE BLACK SATURDAY VICTORIAN BUSHFIRES.

I was shocked and saddened to learn of the terrible toll being exacted by the fires this weekend. I send my heartfelt condolences to the families of all those who have died and my deep sympathy to the many that have lost their homes in this disaster.

On so dreadful an occasion as this for Australia, the fire-fighters and other emergency services have been making extraordinary efforts to contain the situation and tend to those who have been injured. Please also convey to them my renewed admiration for all that they are doing.

Elizabeth R.

This message of deep sympathy was reinforced by the fact she gave a private donation to the Red Cross appeal for bushfire victims.

MESSAGE FROM THE PREMIER

Black Saturday is one of the darkest chapters in Victoria's history.

Too many Victorians lost family, friends and colleagues. Many more lost homes, property and their livelihoods. There have been moments when we could not imagine a more desolate or despairing time for Victoria.

But amid this devastation, we have also seen the very best of human nature.

We have seen unbelievable courage – firefighters and support staff remaining steadfast and doing extraordinary things in the most testing of circumstances. We have seen mateship – tens of thousands of volunteers supporting their communities and doing whatever they can to help. And we have seen incredible resilience and determination – communities coming together and seeking to rebuild in the face of overwhelming loss.

We have also seen amazing generosity – hundreds of thousands of people from across Victoria and around Australia donating money, blood and enough goods to fill the MCG. This united effort from so many individuals and organisations has been inspiring. Victoria will always bear the scars of Black Saturday – but it is the hope and determination of Victorians that will endure as we continue to recover and rebuild.

JOHN BRUMBY MP
Premier of Victoria

CFA IN
ACTION

HOW THE CFA WAS FORMED:

The Country Fire Authority (CFA) was formed in 1945. Volunteer fire brigades have been operating in Victoria since the early 1850's on the goldfields. During the 1890's the Country Fire Brigades Board was formed and the volunteer fire brigade was known as the Rural Fire Brigade. After the disastrous bushfires in 1939 and 1944 which claimed seventy plus lives, the Country Fire Brigade was formed to co-ordinate the different brigades to try and prevent large damaging fires occurring.

HOW THE CFA IS STRUCTURED:

There are over 1,200 brigades in outer metropolitan Melbourne and country Victoria. These brigades are organized into 141 Groups to provide backup for each other when needed. These Brigades and Groups are organized into twenty CFA Regions which are co-ordinated by career fire officers. Every CFA volunteer is put through very extensive training for fire fighting and rescue. Fire fighting is only one part of what the CFA do; they also attend car accidents, floods and every other natural and human disaster! The greatest strength of the CFA is their team work and this is especially seen in times of bushfires where all units are controlled from central control stations, and trucks that leave outer CFA stations are quickly replaced by trucks from other areas and no location is left unprotected. The CFA have lost many members in major bushfires over the years, hence the firefighter's safety is paramount, and they care for each other like a big family.

HOW MANY APPLIANCES AND PERSONNEL DOES THE CFA HAVE?

The CFA is one of the largest fire fighting forces in the world with approximately 58,000 volunteers. These volunteers are supported by more than 400 career firefighters and officers, and over 700 career support and administrative staff.

CFA has over 2,200 vehicles. These include rescue vehicles, fire fighting appliances and personnel protection appliances. The fire trucks are split into two different categories: tankers and pumpers. Tankers are normally four wheel drive vehicles and are used mostly for outer suburban and country areas and have up to a 3,000 litre capacity tank on board. The pumper truck is mostly used in suburban locations and can carry approximately 1,800 litres of water and can pump out between 2,000 to 4,000 litres of water a minute from a fire hydrant or other source. Both trucks carry fire fighting equipment which includes: fire hoses, tools, jacks, axes, a chain saw, rake hoe, spanners, shovels, torches, breathing apparatus, rescue equipment and a fire ladder. These trucks come in different shapes with different water capacities to suit different regions.

THE CFA AND BLACK SATURDAY:

Black Saturday was one of the most trying days for the CFA. They always work very closely with the Bureau of Meteorology, and in the lead up to the 7th of February, there were many warnings being issued to the public by both authorities. When Black Saturday arrived, the CFA was on the highest alert possible, with all hands on deck. The day started quietly and some thought it would be like so many other threatened days that come each summer! This was not to be. As the wind speed and heat rose, the fire danger soared. The CFA took thousands of calls with over 100 significant fires reported over thousands of square kilometres. On Black Saturday there were in excess of 1,700 CFA appliances used, and over 11,700 CFA personnel. The CFA resources were stretched to the limit and they accepted offers of help from fire crews from interstate, and finally overseas.

Most of the CFA is made up of volunteers, and these men and women gave up everything, often including their own families, homes, workplaces and certainly put their own lives in direct danger to protect the people of Victoria that day! Many firefighters had to leave their home to go and defend others' lives and homes with no knowledge of whether their own family or home was safe. Some lost houses and family members whilst saving other people's property.

The people of Victoria have expressed an enormous amount of gratitude to the CFA and other emergency services for their courage and selfless spirit. Many CFA firefighters are unknown and unnamed in public, but that has never lessened the gratefulness that Australians have for the volunteer fire fighting services in this country.

OPERATION
ASSISTANCE

VICTORIA'S CFA WAS EXTREMELY GRATEFUL FOR THE AMOUNT OF HELP RECEIVED FROM OTHER STATES AND COUNTRIES,
SENT TO ASSIST IN FIGHTING THE BUSHFIRES.

NSW alone sent a total of 3652 Rural Fire Service personnel (including Administration Specialists). These were the major contributors of a total of 4600
NSW emergency services personnel, who joined forces to help in the crises that brought the State to its knees.

Sixty specialist fire fighters from the US and ten from Canada also flew in to Melbourne to boost firefighting efforts across the state.

Sadly there was a fatality in the days following Black Saturday when David Balfour, a qualified senior fire fighter from Canberra's ACT fire brigade, was
tragically killed by a falling tree whilst fighting the fires in Victoria.

Two firefighters from NSW, were also injured by falling trees while battling blazes near Alexandra. One of the men was severely hurt with chest and back
injuries, and was taken to Alexandra District Hospital before being air lifted to the Royal Melbourne Hospital. The second man suffered a broken ankle.

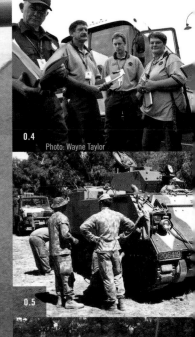

0.2

0.3

0.4

Photo: Wayne Taylor

0.5

0.6

Photo: John Woudstra

0.7

Photo: HWF

0.8

0.1 Members of the NSW Rural Fire Service board an aeroplane to join the fight against the raging bushfires.

0.2 Senior firefighter David Balfour of the ACT Fire Brigade died whilst unselfishly fighting the bushfires.

0.3 Hungry crews arrive for breakfast at the Alexandra staging area for the Murrindindi fires.

0.4 Firefighters arrive from South Australia ready to lend a hand to their neighbouring state.

0.5 The Australian army proved a huge resource in the aftermath and cleanup operations.

0.6 Forestry Tasmania Fire Crew's expertise in fighting mountain wildfires was called upon.

0.7 An ACT firefighter helps out.

0.8 Breaking down the borders, NSW fire teams rushed to help the Victorian fire teams.

DSE BATTLES
THE BLAZE

THE DEPARTMENT OF SUSTAINABILITY AND ENVIRONMENT (DSE) IS VICTORIA'S LEADING GOVERNMENT AGENCY FOR SUSTAINABLE MANAGEMENT OF WATER RESOURCES, CLIMATE CHANGE, BUSHFIRES, PUBLIC LAND, FORESTS AND ECOSYSTEMS.

FIRE MANAGEMENT

Within the context of the Department of Sustainability and Environment's responsibilities, fire management comprises all activities associated with the management of fire prone areas in national parks, state parks and forests. This involves the management of wildfire as well as the use of planned fire on public land to meet land management goals and objectives.

Fire plays an integral role in the management of our parks and forests. Fire management needs to be conducted with an understanding of both the role fire plays in biodiversity maintenance as well as threats it can cause to life and property.

The following statistics show the causes of fires on public land across Victoria and the percentages in each fire category. It is the responsibility of DSE to reduce and prevent the loss of life, property and equipment caused by these fires by implementing planned burning to reduce the fire impacted area.

NUMBER OF FIRES

FIRE CAUSE	AVERAGE NUMBER OF FIRES EACH YEAR	PERCENTAGE OF TOTAL FIRES
Lightning	149	26%
Deliberate	145	25%
Agricultural	96	16%
Campfires	59	10%
Cigarettes/ Matches	41	7%
Miscellaneous	26	5%
Machinery/ Exhausts	15	3%
Planned Burn Escapes *	9	2%
Public Utilities	7	1%
Cause Unknown	37	6%

TOTAL FIRES 584

FEBRUARY FIRES

Despite the efforts of DSE to reduce the toll caused by wildfire, the intensity of the fires of February 2009, and the resulting devastation they caused was never envisaged. Victoria suffered from the worst bushfires in Australia's history, which claimed 173 lives, 2029 homes and 57 businesses.

The state government has responded by allocating a $33.2 million allowance in the state budget to provide new equipment for DSE, among other initiatives.

As a result of the February fires, Victoria has been left with a cost of almost $1 billion associated with the fighting of the fires. The costs incurred by DSE, MFB, CFA and interstate and overseas firefighters amounted to $344 million.

The DSE responded on Black Saturday with the due diligence that would be expected of it. They worked closely with the CFA and other emergency Government departments. The DSE had been fighting the fires in the Bunyip State Park in the week leading into Black Saturday. These crews had fought day & night and had often had to fight the fire in areas inaccessible to vehicles, which meant they had long marches to the firefront carrying their fire fighting kits with them which sometimes included heavy rakes, to beat the flames in grassland. When Saturday 7th February started getting out of control, these crews were stretched to the absolute limit, and mainly worked with the CFA concentrating on asset protection.

On Black Saturday, the DSE committed 3,400 members to fighting the fires, which included 4WD slip-on fire fighting ute crews, bulldozer crews, tanker truck crews, operational staff, support staff, fire spotters and many other personnel as well. In total there were 2,600 kilometres of control lines built by fire crews during the 2009 fire season.

The people of Victoria have expressed their gratitude to the DSE for their exhausting work carried out during Black Saturday, often endangering their own lives to save others. One such DSE member was the fire spotter seated high above the flames in the Mount Gordon fire spotter tower. As the fire storm raced toward him, he rang many members of the public and other emergency authorities to warn them of the coming disaster. This man only just escaped himself before the fire swept through the bottom of the tower. Many DSE members are unsung heroes to whom many owe their lives.

THE AIR
ATTACK

A large bushfire such as Black Saturday involves co-operation between a large number of departments within the CFA and the DSE. The Country Fire Authority's (CFA) local firestations are based in country townships, as well as around the perimeter of major cities where bushland, farms and forests abut the built-up housing areas of the city fringe. The CFA is responsible for fighting fires on private property, whilst the Department of Sustainability and Environment (DSE) is responsible for fires on public land, such as National Parks and State Forests. Obviously there is an overlap between the two departments.

LOCAL RESPONSE

When a fire is reported to '000', the call is diverted by the emergency centre to Vicfire who are responsible for notifying the DSE or local CFA in the area concerned. The Fire Captain and other brigade crew are then alerted by pagers, and the fire alarm siren is automatically activated, alerting townspeople of the approaching fire. The CFA then responds by sending one or more fire trucks, depending on the size of the incident reported. A strike team consisting of five fire trucks is then deployed in major fires which typically consist of trucks from neighbouring areas. They then rendezvous at a predetermined location, ready to work together on a fire outbreak. The first truck at the scene is responsible to assess the fire, and the captain or 2IC (Second in Command) then calls Vicfire for more appliances, including aircraft support if needed. The Captain then takes command of the fire and is known as the IC (Incident Controller). If the fire increases in intensity, Vicfire pages more CFA brigades to respond, and upgrades the fire level.

AIRCRAFT SUPPORT

Vicfire then rings the Regional Duty Officer (RDO) in the CFA region concerned, who contacts the State Aircraft Unit (SAU) for aircraft support. The SAU is part of the CFA's emergency response management, who then deploys the water bombing aircraft, under the command of the Air Attack Supervisor (AAS) who is on call 24/7. The AAS immediately responds by commanding helicopter crews on standby, to action.

The large Canadian-based Erikson Air Cranes, such as Elvis and Bluey, two of the most powerful firefighting helicopters in the world, then leap into action. They are on 15 minute standby, ready for service 24 hours a day during high fire risk seasons.

Once the AAS and the water bombing helicopters are airborne, the air desk communications officer based at the IECC (Integrated Emergency Control Centre), in Nicholson St, Melbourne, advises details of the flight and all personnel involved. Every 30 minutes thereafter until flight completion, there is a call made to the air desk updating flight progress.

The water bombing helicopter then finds a suitable water filling location in the vicinity of the fire, and fills the tank with a hose hanging from the helicopter into the water supply (dam or lake). The water often looks a dark murky colour due to the muddy water from dams.

Meanwhile, the AAS flies ahead into the fire area and corresponds with the Incident Controller based in a fire truck at the scene. The IC then confirms the most urgent location for water bombing, such as saving a house. Once the location is identified, the AAS guides the water bomber to the drop zone. After ground crews clear the drop zone, the AAS gives an all-clear signal to the water bomber to "Come in and Drop".

The water bombing helicopters are totally at the command of the AAS, who is in constant contact with ground attack crews, Incident Control Centre and the Air Desk. The water bombing crew is ever mindful of the inherent dangers surrounding their tasks; power lines, radiant heat and surrounding obstacles, including communication towers, etc.

The flight must be terminated within 10 minutes of last light after sundown, which is predetermined by the helicopter's equipment.

Helicorp provided a vital link in the aerial defence of the February fires in Victoria, assisting the DSE and CFA to save property, lives, houses and buildings. Brave pilots water bombed locations that could not be accessed easily, in time frames impossible for vehicles on land. The quantity of water dropped at one time, undoubtedly saved lives that would have been lost without these invaluable aircraft.

SES TO THE
RESCUE

THE VICTORIAN STATE EMERGENCY SERVICE (SES) IS A VOLUNTEER BASED EMERGENCY SERVICE, OPERATING THROUGHOUT THE STATE OF VICTORIA.

SES responds to a wide range of emergencies including floods, severe storms, earthquakes, road accident rescue as well as search and rescue. You can often see SES teams hard at work in the middle of the night using chainsaws to cut up fallen trees that have broken through a house roof or blocking a roadway. Their expertise in assisting at major road accidents using the jaws of life to prise open severely damaged vehicles has regularly been a contributor to a trapped occupant's life being saved. It also provides a support role to other emergency services with more than 5,500 volunteers across the state.

SES also provides support and guidance to Government departments and municipalities, and is responsible for an audit role on all municipal emergency plans. The Victoria State Emergency Service assists in countering the effects of natural and technological emergencies and supports Victoria's emergency management arrangements through planning and preparedness activities.

SES volunteers played an integral part in Victoria's bushfire event, providing support to the CFA and DSE, Victoria Police, DHS and Red Cross in the form of personnel and resources.

More than 1,000 SES volunteers and staff across the state were involved in the fire support activities. SES assumed a significant role at the relief centres, assisting Red Cross with the coordination of donations, and they were operating in the IECC (Incident Emergency Control Centre) 24 hours a day, and continued this throughout the whole week after Black Saturday. They were also heavily involved with chainsaw crews and ground observers, as well as transporting supplies and crews whilst providing essential resources for staging areas and relief centres, including lighting towers, vehicles, shelter resources and equipment. Taskforces from all over the state were deployed to assist with loss and damage assessment, traffic management points and clearing trees from roadways. Over the weekend of 7th February, SES attended to over 340 tasks statewide, with over 40 units and 290 volunteers involved.

SES was heavily involved in the setting up and running of base camps at Healesville, Alexandra and Wesburn. Each base camp accommodated up to 500 firefighters, providing accommodation and catering alongside the staging area. South Australia SES provided base camp managers and incident management teams for each camp, supported by local SES volunteers from nearby units.

A multi-agency taskforce was also involved in helping remove persons from collapsed structures in support of DVI (Disaster Victim Identification unit) teams.

In many areas, including Kinglake, the fires were so fast that SES and other emergency departments barely had time to respond to the crises before the fires were on them. The Kinglake SES building reflected this story, as it was burnt down with the two SES vehicles still behind the closed doors of the building. They weren't even able to get the vehicles on the road before the building was overrun by flames.

The SES did a magnificent job on Black Saturday and it has always been a highly respected organization for their life saving management in their service to the people of Victoria.

Vehicles at the Kinglake SES station never made it out!

BLACK SATURDAY'S
POLICE RESPONSE

WHEN PEOPLE RANG 000 FOR POLICE ASSISTANCE ON BLACK SATURDAY IT WAS ANSWERED BY D24 POLICE COMMUNICATIONS CENTRE. THEY RECEIVED 3586 CALLS ON SATURDAY 7TH FEBRUARY AND 3578 THE FOLLOWING DAY.

IT TOOK A TOTAL OF 82,267 CALLS THROUGHOUT FEBRUARY, ANSWERING 86.4 PERCENT OF CALLS WITHIN FIVE SECONDS. THE PRESSURE ON THE CALL CENTRE WAS INTENSE DUE TO THE CALLERS BEING IN AN EXTREMELY DISTRESSED STATE AND FEARFUL FOR THEIR LIVES.

The radio network in Marysville had broken down and D24 helped re-establish the radio network, providing a communications base after fires destroyed the transmission towers. It was also responsible for installing two radio channels to assist coverage around Kinglake and Kilmore.

Police had trained for this type of disaster in the hope that they would never have to put those plans into action. The Black Saturday fires took just hours to explode, but they destroyed so much. They were years in the making with twelve years of drought and dry weather conditions, coupled with extreme temperatures and gale force winds that combined to create this disaster.

Photo: HWT

Photo: HWT

Photo: HWT

As Kieran Walsh (deputy commissioner) stood before a packed media contingent around 9:30pm on Saturday 7th February he confirmed the news some predicted but no one wanted to hear.

Reporters were informed that fourteen people were dead and it was feared that figure could stretch into the forties following the bushfires across Victoria, many of which were still burning. The full extent of the tragedy would not become known for days, but many people would lose their lives, thousands of homes would be destroyed, and 400,000 hectares of land devastated. It would become evident in the days following that this was Australia's worst ever natural disaster and the first gruelling 48 hours would signal the start of a week of horrific trauma.

AUSTRALIA'S WORST EVER NATURAL DISASTER

As news of the State's worst ever natural disaster broke on a stunned world that Saturday afternoon, national and international media agencies bombarded the Victoria Police with 14,683 calls during February. Ten experienced media officers from interstate assisted the Victorian police media department in their huge demand.

Up to 600 police were brought in from other regions to assist with the workload, whilst army personnel and police from other states, as well as New Zealand and Indonesia, were flown in to assist the Disaster Victim Identification unit.

One major problem facing the police, was that if fire affected areas were to receive an unseasonable dump of rain; there could be unprecedented mudslides and floods due to a buildup of ash deposits and the lack of live foliage.

Police were under incredible pressure as they directed traffic and worked to save lives in fire affected areas around the state.

At Kinglake Police station, a call came in during the afternoon alerting them of a four-car pileup on the Whittlesea–Kinglake Road. They made their way to the site in two separate police cars only to be driven back by flames. Eventually, when they arrived at the scene, they found one person trapped who had died in the flames. To make it worse the victim was known to the police officers who attended. Many victims indentified through the next few days were known by police in these tight knit communities, which was a demoralizing and stifling drain on them and other local emergency personnel in the immediate areas.

Another call came through at 6:30pm that Saturday evening alerting police of fifteen children trapped at Kinglake West Primary School. Police officers responded only to realise later it was a false alarm and they only narrowly escaped the burning entrance themselves after checking the building.

Many police on duty that afternoon did a non-stop 24 hour shift. It was only their adrenalin that kept them going in the face of the crises.

After the fires, came the grisly task of identifying victims. Along debris littered roads lined with charred trees and gutted ruins of homes, there were blue and white ribbons wrapped around entrances to houses, around the burnt out remains of cars and specific locations where persons lost their lives.

Even weeks after the fires had stopped burning, amidst the once tree lined streets, there were figures dressed in the white uniforms of the Disaster Victim Identification unit (DVI) standing out amongst the black surrounds. They worked tirelessly in groups of four to six sifting through the ash and rubble to identify any human remains they found.

A FAMILY HUDDLED TOGETHER IN THE CORNER

For days and days following the fires, police had up to eighteen teams with many working 16 hour shifts, piecing together the jigsaw puzzles. "It was an adrenalin fuelled project where everyone wanted to help," said Sergeant Trevor Blake of the DVI Unit. "Our members have seen some horrific gut-wrenching sights. One unforgettable memory was a dead family huddled

The members also had to keep a close eye on each other whilst working on this kind of job. Every bit of support and encouragement from team members was greatly appreciated and helped lift morale amongst the crew.

There were four phases of the DVI process put into action immediately following the fires and a fifth debriefing phase at the end of each incident.

DISASTER VICTIM IDENTIFICATION PROCESS

Phase One-Involves the search for victims and the collection, documentation and photography of remains at the scene.

Phase Two-The victim is taken to a mortuary where the remains are examined

Phase Three-DNA, fingerprint, medical and dental samples are taken from relatives of the victims as well as physical descriptions.

Phase Four-The remains collected in phase one are linked to the samples collected in phases two and three and the information is presented to the Coroner so the victim can be formally identified.

Phase Five-All members of the unit involved are debriefed on the incident. Roads and Public areas were searched first, then houses with collapsed structures which needed the assistance of heavy machinery to help with the clearing. Once clearing work was completed, the teams sifted through the rubble to locate any further victims.

DOWN ON HANDS AND KNEES SIFTING THROUGH ASHES

It took days at times just to move rubble and go through an area, a scene where members were down on their hands and knees sifting through the ashes to recover anything that might provide clues in the search.

Some of the fires appear to have been deliberately lit and are treated as crime scenes. Coordination between the police dog squad, search and rescue crew as well as Forensic experts was invaluable.

Dog and handler teams were used in the early stages to check for signs of life. Alsatians trained in the recovery of bodies wore special shoes to ensure embers wouldn't burn their paws as they worked methodically over each search site. Fifty-three teams of two detectives were finally given the massive task of collating the majority of information which was then presented to the coroner.

THE POLICE AIR-WING

The Police Air-wing was used in intensive rescue missions on Black Saturday. The police helicopter crew was involved in winching persons out of remote clearings in the middle of heavily treed locations. Incidents like this occurred just forward of the main firefront with only minutes to spare.

The gale force winds hampered their efforts and it was only the incredibly skilful piloting of the jet assisted helicopters that enabled people's lives to be saved. The winch line was blown at angles of up to 45° with the wild wind speed (up to 150 kilometres per hour), that was throwing the Helicopter and winch line from side to side as well as up and down by at least five metres every second or two. The Pilot battled nature's fury to stay safe distances from obstacles whilst trying to drop the winch line within grasp of the person being rescued. Some of these operations were like mission impossible and had to be aborted at times to avoid any uncertain outcomes. These situations created life and death decisions either way and the responsibility on the officers involved in these life saving exercises was enormous.

AMBULANCE SERVICE
SAVES LIVES

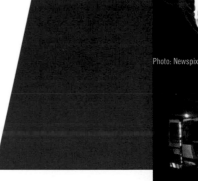
Photo: Newspix

THE AMBULANCE SERVICE STARTED IN VICTORIA IN ABOUT 1883 AND HAS SERVED THE PEOPLE SELFLESSLY EVER SINCE.

Ambulance Victoria has always worked closely with all Victorian emergency services as it is able to respond to any natural disaster or crises that occur.

From its humble beginnings back in 1883 it has steadily grown and now has more than 200 strategically located branches across Victoria and a dedicated staff of 2,500 operational ambulance paramedics across all skill levels. In addition to this, Ambulance Victoria also has 300 non-operational staff who help run the administrative and managerial side of the service.

When the horror of Black Saturday started to unfold, the ambulance service swung into action immediately. They closely liaised with the CFA, police and other Government agencies so they were available at the right location at the correct time.

Due to the extreme circumstances of the day it was not always easy to be everywhere at once, so Ambulance Victoria set up bases close to the fires hoping to be in the best possible position to help people as they arrived, in whatever state they came in. Air Ambulance Victoria worked closely with the police, airlifting people as quickly as possible to hospitals in the city for emergency treatment

Each medical base had an ambulance group manager, a senior intensive care paramedic, and other paramedics.

It also had an emergency support crew capable of treating 200 people. They had a large supply of medical equipment, thus providing a comprehensive first aid service to the victims of the fire.

Ambulance Victoria worked tirelessly all of Black Saturday, through the night and for many days afterwards. Many ambulance officers saw terrible sights of both physical and emotional suffering that day, which has had an effect on many officers for life.

The people of Victoria are forever grateful for the tireless work and attention that Ambulance Victoria devotes to them at all times, especially in times of calamity such as Black Saturday.

RED CROSS

FEBRUARY 2009 SAW BUSHFIRES SWEEP ACROSS VICTORIA ON AN UNPRECEDENTED SCALE. THE WORST NATURAL DISASTER IN AUSTRALIA'S HISTORY CLAIMED 173 LIVES, WITH THE HIGHEST DEATH TOLL ON 7 FEBRUARY. THE FIRES ALSO CLAIMED THE HOMES OF MORE THAN 2000 FAMILIES, LEFT MORE THAN 7000 PEOPLE HOMELESS, DESTROYED HUNDREDS OF THOUSANDS OF HECTARES OF LAND AND TRAUMATISED AND SCATTERED COMMUNITIES.

RED CROSS RELIEF EFFORTS

More than 1000 Red Cross people worked around the clock at 20 relief centres state-wide to help survivors. At the peak of relief efforts, Red Cross volunteers and staff worked to reconnect loved ones, support the evacuated and the distressed, and provide information and referrals to specialised services.

Over a period of four weeks following the fires, 20,000 people registered with Red Cross volunteers at relief centres, by phone or email to let loved ones know they were safe. Over the same period, Red Cross volunteers responded to 21,000 enquiries from concerned family and friends. This registration process is part of the National Registration and Inquiry System, designed to reunite families and friends separated by emergencies and provide news of their whereabouts and safety to concerned enquirers. During significant emergencies, Red Cross establishes an inquiry centre for all enquiries from the public. As was the case during this emergency, the system is a critical tool in police victim identification.

Red Cross first aid volunteers at relief centres were kept busy providing more than 5250 first aid treatments and Red Cross catering volunteers cooked more than 200,000 meals for evacuees and emergency services personnel in affected areas.

Together with the Victorian and Federal Governments, Red Cross established the Victorian Bushfires Appeal 2009 on 8 February. The community spirit and response was staggering. More than 500,000 people locally and internationally donated to the Appeal, which has raised more than $370 million – the most generous outpouring of financial support this nation has ever seen. A remarkable response during difficult economic times.

ALL FUNDS RAISED ARE BEING DISTRIBUTED THROUGH THE DEPARTMENT OF HUMAN SERVICES UNDER THE OVERSIGHT OF AN INDEPENDENT ADVISORY PANEL. MORE THAN $120 MILLION HAS ALREADY BEEN DISTRIBUTED THROUGH PAYMENTS FROM THE FUND, WHICH INCLUDE:

- compassion and bereavement payments
- rebuilding and recovery payments (tenants)
- initial home dislocation payments
- exceptional hardship support payments
- severe injury payments
- local government relief payments
- household repairs payments

- rural properties recovery assistance payments
- tools of trade payments
- severe injury transition to home payments
- rebuilding and recovery payments (destroyed)
- winter needs payments
- rebuilding and recovery payments (damaged)
- winter community events packages.

MOVING INTO RECOVERY

The short to medium term phase of recovery involves sustaining temporary arrangements and making a start on rebuilding homes, lives and communities. Linking people with services, lending an ear and trying to get people back to a normal sense of things are ways Red Cross continues to provide support as residents come to terms with the magnitude of this disaster.

Recovery centres and community service hubs have replaced relief centres, ensuring people are able to access all bushfire-related services in a central place and remain supported throughout their recovery.

Red Cross continues to monitor the recovery effort and has undertaken outreach activities and even door-to-door home visiting to check on people's well-being. Red Cross has a team of people working with communities over the next 12 months and beyond to deliver recovery services and activities that will best help people to get back on their own feet. Red Cross will continue to identify what it can do to support communities in their recovery and will negotiate to undertake new roles as required.

Red Cross will also continue as a member of the Independent Advisory Panel overseeing distribution of Bushfire Appeal funds to ensure assistance reaches individuals and communities affected by these devastating fires.

AUSTRALIAN RED CROSS AND THE GENERAL PUBLIC CAME TOGETHER IN A TRUE DEMONSTRATION OF SUPPORT ...
THAT'S THE POWER OF HUMANITY.

RESPONSE FROM
THE SALVATION ARMY

THE SALVATION ARMY IS A WORLDWIDE CHRISTIAN MOVEMENT. IN AUSTRALIA WE ARE KNOWN AS ONE OF THE NATION'S LARGEST WELFARE PROVIDERS. WE ARE DEDICATED TO HELPING AUSTRALIANS IN CRISIS, GIVEN THAT CENTRAL TO OUR MISSION IS HELPING TO TRANSFORM LIVES, CARING FOR PEOPLE, AND ADVOCATING AND WORKING FOR THE REFORMING OF SOCIETY.

Each year The Salvation Army assists more than one million people; our core areas of work include assisting families facing crisis, family and domestic violence, homelessness and addiction services.

The Salvation Army has been heavily involved in providing support to Victorians affected by the bushfires of Black Saturday, 7th February.

The Salvation Army was on the ground providing aid to communities within hours of the first fires commencing, as well as supporting the emergency service teams battling the fires that raged for weeks. During the critical response phase of operations, The Salvation Army served more than 40,000 meals, and provided immediate financial assistance, personal and emotional support to thousands involved in the Victorian bushfires.

The Salvation Army is now partnering with other agencies, government groups, churches and local communities. We are working with 28 newly formed Community Recovery Committees, that have been established to develop plans and projects that will aid the recovery of specific communities and the rebuilding process.

With the support from generous members of the public and corporate community, The Salvation Army has been able to make a difference to the lives of thousands of people affected by bushfire. Six months after Black Saturday we have distributed more than $8 million in aid to affected communities and are continually looking for appropriate ways to support the recovery process.

Working towards long-term support strategies, The Salvation Army is expanding its role to provide care and support for individuals, families and communities and local small businesses.

Each week, more than 500 people come to Salvation Army Bushfire Recovery Centres for assistance.

Since Black Saturday, The Salvation Army has helped more than 4,000 people with more than 12,000 contacts made at their centres.

The Salvation Army has distributed more than 48,000 vouchers to those affected by the fires.

Twenty cars and caravans have been provided through the Salvos by the generosity of the public. More than 900 volunteers assisted The Salvation Army in their response to the bushfires.

THE BUSHFIRE'S IMPACT ON
ANIMALS

ONE ASPECT OF BUSHFIRES OFTEN OVERLOOKED IS THE DEVASTATING IMPACT IT HAS ON OUR NATIVE FAUNA, BUT THE NUMBER OF ANIMALS THAT PERISHED ON BLACK SATURDAY COULD NEVER BE QUANTIFIED.

Such was the speed and ferocity of the firestorm that swept across the state that koalas couldn't outclimb it, kangaroos couldn't outjump it, echidnas couldn't outburrow it, hares couldn't outrun it and many birds couldn't even outfly it.

The magnitude of injured and wounded animals soon became evident at wildlife shelters around the areas which had fallen victim to the raging conflagration. Casualties including kangaroos, koalas and a vast range of pets with burnt paws and fur, were amongst the influx of rescued animals rushed to wildlife shelters and veterinary surgeries. Volunteers worked round the clock to keep tiny hearts pumping, and provide whatever comfort they could to the sufferers of the animal kingdom.

Scores of farmers also took a blow as unfortunate livestock became trapped in paddocks bordered by fences that were usually there for their safety. Running blindly through the smoke, trying to find an escape route that wasn't there, countless livestock perished as they became captives in their own comfort zone or ensnared on the wire barriers. Pitiful scenes such as these were commonplace in the days following the inferno.

Survival is number one on an animal's list of priorities and many animal species, including those of a shyer nature, drew closer to mankind in the weeks after the bushfires. Food and drink were clearly main concerns. One koala was even seen leaning over a private swimming pool, at full stretch, in an effort to secure a much needed drink and satisfy its thirsting body.

Photo: HWT

Photo: HWT

Photo: HWT

Photo: HWT

Photo: Sebastian Costanzo

Photo: Newspix

Photo: Help for Wildlife

Photo: Newspix

Photo: Newspix

Photo: Newspix

2009 VICTORIAN BUSHFIRES
ROYAL COMMISSION

Directly after the 7th February 'Black Saturday' bushfires, the Premier of Victoria, the Hon John Brumby, called for a Royal Commission to be established immediately to look into the bushfires with a view to never again see such unparalleled loss of human life, wildlife and property.

Although bushfires are a fact of life in Australia, ways need to be investigated to preserve life and properties as much as possible.

The 2009 Victorian Bushfires Royal Commission was established on 16th February 2009 to investigate the causes of, preparation for, and responses to the Victorian Bushfires, which swept through parts of Victoria in late January and February 2009 and the impact of the fires on infrastructure.

The Commission is chaired by the Hon. Bernard Teague AO, supported by Commissioners Ron McLeod AM and Susan Pascoe AM.

COMMUNITY ENGAGEMENT

The Commission's first priority was to meet and listen to people directly affected by the fires. Between 18th March 2009 and 9th April 2009 the Commission held 26 Community Consultations in 14 fire affected locations attended by 1256 local people. The sessions were professionally facilitated and counselling support was available. Scribes captured small group discussions and plenary reporting was videotaped for the use of the Royal Commission.

A total of 87 witnesses, including 29 lay witnesses, have given evidence during 35 days of public hearings.

"The primary focus of this block of hearings was on dealing with issues to give us a better understanding of what happened on the seventh of February and to use this knowledge to help create a safer environment for Victorians before the next fire season," said the Chair, Commissioner Bernard Teague. Commissioner Susan Pascoe said she had been moved and inspired by the stories of courage and heroism that had emerged from the hearings and she particularly praised the efforts of emergency service personnel.

"We should never forget the efforts of many CFA volunteers, some of whom left their own homes at risk to go and fight fires on that terrible day," she said. "There were also police officers, and other members of the community, who showed remarkable courage."

The Royal Commission into Victoria's Black Saturday bushfires has heard the fires were as powerful as 1,500 atomic bombs the size of the one dropped on Hiroshima. Fire ecologist, Dr Kevin Tolhurst from the University of Melbourne prepared a report for the commission that mapped the progression and severity of the February 7th fires. In Dr Kevin Tolhurst's report were some of the starkest statements of what man faced on Black Saturday.

His report found the fires gave off the energy equivalent to that used by Victoria in one year, saying that people would need to be at least 150 metres from such flames to remain safe, and the Black Saturday fires were so powerful that they created their own weather conditions and their own microclimates, sometimes causing wind drafts of up to 120 kilometres per hour which were powerful enough to snap trees.

He also said that most of the damage done by bushfires happens after the arrival of a cool change, saying there was a cool change on February 7th which was "the worst situation we could have."

INTERIM REPORT

Bushfires Royal Commission: the recommendations August 17, 2009.

Among the recommendations made by the Bushfires Royal Commission were:

STAY OR GO

Victorians will be told that leaving early is always the safest way to survive a bushfire and that not all homes are defensible. Children should not stay behind with other family members if residents choose to stay to try and defend their homes. If a household decides to stay they should have a back-up plan and be ready to relocate to a fire refuge if necessary.

WARNINGS

Bushfire warnings will be designed to save as many lives as possible. Warnings will be split into two categories - bushfire information and bushfire warnings - to emphasise when a fire has become an imminent danger. Warnings will provide clear information on the location and expected path of a fire and time-frames for when communities could expect to be affected. Establish a national telephone-based warning system, including a new fire severity scale to clearly warn communities of the level of danger they are in. Ensure the Standard Emergency Warning Signal is used to precede the most serious bushfire warnings when broadcast. Commercial broadcasters, not just the ABC, will be able to broadcast official bushfire warnings. Guidelines will be developed for the use of fire sirens in communities to warn residents of bushfires. The Fire Danger Index which rates the intensity of a fire would be included in fire weather warnings issued by the Bureau of Meteorology. The index was designed to reach 100 but on Black Saturday registered 328. Victims of the fires told the commission they believed they should have been told the fire index to give them a clearer idea of the danger they faced.

A single website would combine CFA and DSE warnings and information. The commission has recommended that the CFA chief be responsible for warning communities of approaching bushfires.

REFUGES

Neighbourhood safe places and community refuges will be identified and advertised to residents and visitors in high-risk towns to provide shelter to people unable to flee. Local Government will be responsible for the designation of emergency relief centres in case relocations are necessary. The CFA will prioritise defending community fire refuges when they are in use.

RELOCATIONS

The current stay or go policy would be overhauled to ensure its focus is on protecting lives and the term 'relocation' be used in preference to 'evacuation'. CFA staff would be able to advise particular households, locations or communities whether they believed it would be safer for them to go than stay. Incident controllers will be required to assess whether people should relocate and if necessary to recommend residents leave their properties.

It is illegal under Victorian law to force a person who has a pecuniary interest in a land or building under threat to leave the property because of a fire danger. The Commission's Final Report is due to be completed by 31st July next year.

Information in this document represents the interim findings of the Royal Commission which might change when the final report is released. They were correct at time of publishing.

A GUIDE TO
SURVIVAL

For more information go to the CFA website on www.cfa.vic.gov.au or call the Victorian Bushfire Information Line on 1800 240 667

AUSTRALIA WILL ALWAYS HAVE BUSHFIRES, BUT PROPER PLANNING AND SAFETY PROCEDURES CAN LIMIT THE RISK TO PROPERTY AND LIFE. THIS GUIDE EXPLAINS HOW YOU CAN PROTECT YOUR FAMILY AND HOUSE.

SCREEN OUT THE FIRE
Fitting ordinary metal flyscreens to your windows can save your home by cutting down the amount of radiant heat on the windows, preventing them from cracking during a fire, and also keeping out embers. Screens should also be used on outside doors, vents and chimneys to keep out embers. Similarly, any other cracks through which embers can enter the house should be sealed. Don't let sparks enter through broken windows. Ventilation louveres in the roof should be lined from inside with metal flywire screening.

VERANDAS, PERGOLAS, CARPORTS AND DECKS
Any combustible veranda, pergola or deck should be:
- adequately separated dwelling by noncombustible materials to prevent fire spread.
- Provided with gaps between decking materials for embers to fall through.

LEAF-FREE GUTTERS
Leaves in the gutters help fire get into the roof. They need to be kept clean throughout summer. Fitting leaf guards or a leafless guttering system will help to keep guttering clear. Block gaps with non-combustible material such as compressed mineral fibre.

MULCH
Use decayed humus mulch instead of woodchip or dry straw. Keep it moist.

VEGETATION NEAR THE HOUSE
Make sure all vegetation around the house is pruned (especially lower branches), kept tidy and does not overhang the house. Take out small saplings (vulnerable to fire) and mow the lawns with a mower fitted with a grass catcher. Rake up any grass or leaves in the yard that might serve as fuel for a fire. Contact your local council before destroying, lopping or removing any plants as you may require a permit.

ROOF SPACE SAFETY
Cracks in roof tiles can allow embers into the roof space of the house, causing a fire above the ceiling. To reduce this risk lay fire resistantmaterial or aluminium foil between the roof covering (including tiles, sheet metal) and the rafters.

DO NOT STAND ON THE ROOF DURING A BUSHFIRE – STRONG WIND DURING FIRES CAN BE DANGEROUS

Block downpipes and fill gutters with water before the fire arrives

Fire wood

Flammable Rubbish

Weather strips on doorways

Petrol Pump

HANDY WATER
At points of the house where embers might collect clear debris away regularly and watch for embers regularly as the firefront approaches and after it has passed. Keep a hose or metal buckets of water and mops handy to extinguish the embers.

HOW HOUSES BURN DOWN DURING A BUSHFIRE

fireready **VICTORIA**

AROUND & UNDER THE HOUSE
Clear away any potential fuel for a fire, such as bushes, leaves, grass and wood from around and under the house. Remove any other combustible items such as doormats or garden furniture from near the house.

INDEPENDENT WATER SOURCE
An independent water source such as a swimming pool, tank or dam provides an important reservoir of water. If you are on a mains supply, do not rely on it during a bushfire. A non-electric pump could be used to operate hoses and sprinklers in the event of mains pressure failure.

LP GAS BOTTLES
Make sure that the gas bottles are set in a solid concrete base and fixed to a strong metal pipe that is not under a veranda, that the pressure relief valve is pointing away from the house and that the area around the bottle is cleared of flammable material for at least six metres.

DURING A BUSHFIRE OR A GRASS FIRE, A HOUSE CAN BE SET ALIGHT IN THREE WAYS:

- Embers and burning debris carried by the wind
- Radiant heat from the fire
- Flames directly touching the house

Research consistently shows embers are the main way houses are set alight during bushfires. Ember attack can best be described as the small burning twigs and leaves that are carried ahead of the main fire. They land on and around houses before the main firefront arrives. These small burning twigs and leaves can land in roof gutters, or timber verandas, on doormats or on other combustible material close to the house and may smoulder for many hours. Without anyone to extinguish these small fires, they gradually get larger and spread to other parts of the building and its contents until the whole building becomes engulfed in fire. Burning embers may land on a house during all stages of the fire – before the firefront arrives, during the passage of the firefront and for many hours after the main firefront has passed. This is why it is important to continue to patrol around the house for burning embers up to six hours (and sometimes longer) after the main fire has passed through. It is during this time that many houses burn down.

Radiant heat can ignite timber on a building only when a lot of fuel such as forest-like vegetation, overgrown gardens, and other buildings burn quite close to the building. However, radiant heat plays a significant role in heating up fuel so that ignition by embers or flame is easier. Radiant heat can also crack or break windows, allowing embers to enter, and plastics such as wall cladding can be distorted badly or melted to expose timber framing. Most serious is the exposure of people to radiant heat. The amount of direct flame contact and/or radiant heat a house may be subjected to depends on how far the house is from the source of the heat. If the distance from the fire is doubled, the radiant heat load on the building can be reduced by up to four times.

Wind

Crown

Rising Heat

Ground Fire

Surface Fire

Burning leaves, bark and twigs, known as embers, are blown forward with the wind. This provides an ignition source for fuel ahead of the main fire. These initially small fires are called spot fires. Loose, flaky or ribbon bark often found on eucalypts can contribute significantly to ember attack and long distance spotting.

DON'T YOU BE THE ONE TO START THE FIRE!

Know your responsibilities during the fire period:

- Do not burn off without a permit
- Check conditions before welding and grinding
- Take care with your vehicle on roadsides
- Dispose of cigarettes carefully
- Fully extinguish campfires

Take special care on days of Total Fire Ban

DON'T GET CAUGHT OUT ON THE ROADS

- Smoke ahead? U-turn to safety!
- Avoid driving in areas where there is fire activity.
- During a bushfire, roads are extremely dangerous.

If caught on the road during a bushfire:

- don't get out of the car and run.
- pull over in a cleared area.
- put headlights and hazard lights on.
- shut windows and vents and get below window level.
- cover exposed skin but not with synthetic material.
- when fire has passed, get out of the car.

DON'T EXPECT A FIRE TRUCK
CFA will attend every fire but may not get to every house
Plan to be on your own in a bushfire
Prepare and practice your bushfire survival plan now!

WHAT TO WEAR

- Wide-brimmed hat or hard helmet
- Goggles to protect eyes from smoke and ash
- Towel or face mask tied around nose and mouth to filter smoke
- Long-sleeved overalls or long-sleeved wool or cotton shirt to protect skin from radiant heat
- Sturdy gloves made of natural fibre, not rubber or synthetic
- Sturdy shoes or boots with thick leather soles
- Long, natural fibre pants such as jeans, which will not melt

LEAVING EARLY

CFA recommends that people make their decision well before the summer fire season to either stay and actively defend their property or to leave the area before the fire threatens. If you decide to leave your home you must do so before a fire threatens and road travel becomes hazardous. If a fire is burning nearby, late evacuation can be a deadly option.

Once the fire is close, there will be a lot of smoke in the area; visibility will be very poor and road travel will be hazardous. Fallen trees, power lines, abandoned cars or even firefighting vehicles may block roads. Most importantly, you will be exposing yourself to the dangers of radiant heat.

Experience has shown that many residents receive little, if any, official warning of an approaching fire.

The very nature of a bushfire is that it may threaten your property within minutes of starting, before you have received any warning.

You may not have time to leave the area safely and you may not know which direction the fire is traveling. Your house offers better protection from the heat of the fire than being in your car in the open.

YOUR SAFETY KIT

- Medicines
- Spare clothes (cotton fabrics)
- Sturdy shoes
- Torch with new batteries
- Hat and sunscreen
- Water bottle, light snacks, baby formula
- Animal carrier and leads

TREASURE BOX

- Passport and driver's licence
- Title deeds
- Marriage/birth certificates
- Medical records
- Insurance/business papers
- Wedding photos
- Jewellery and trophies
- Credit cards
- University diplomas
- Files, documents, computer disks

REMEMBER!

- Do not rely on your electricity supply. It will probably fail.
- You will not get an official warning to leave. This is your decision.

ACKNOWLEDGEMENTS

When we come to thanking and acknowledging all those who contributed to the Firestorm publication we feel distinctly inadequate to convey our appreciation fully. This book is not written by one person or a group of persons, it is written by a community. It is written by previously unknown persons, victims of tragedy, survivors, commentators, local people, community leaders, emergency personnel. It is not an inquest into the fires. It is a coalescence of stories, pictures, experiences, dramas, ponderings and reminiscences from a recovering community that have united to provide a moving memento of the firestorm that was Saturday 7th February, 2009.

Sincere gratitude is extended to all those who were so ready to share and contribute and donate material for the book. Thank you for taking your part in the healing process.

**STORIES, PHOTOGRAPHS,
REFERENCE MATERIAL & GRAPHICS**

We are very thankful for the support we received from the Government and the authorities including information, letters and messages.

In particular we would like to thank:
Her Majesty, Queen Elizabeth II
The Honourable Kevin Rudd, Prime Minister of Australia
John Brumby MP, Premier of Victoria
We would also like to acknowledge our appreciation of input courtesy of the following organizations & individuals:
ACT Emergency Services Agency
Agence France Presse
Allen, Malcome & Michelle
Amatnieks, Karl & Jayne
Ambulance Victoria
Associated Press
Atkinson, Rod
Australian Federal Police
Azzopardi, Charlie
Baruta, Jim
Bayliss, Jane
Brown, Peter
Brown, Ted
Bureau of Meteorology
Bursill, Sharon
Cameron, Lisa
Cadman, Tanya
CFA pix
Channel 9
Channel 10
Cimo, Bruno
Commin, John
Commisso, Luke
Corr, Pat
Country Fire Authority (CFA)
Crystal Graphics
Dallinger, Simon
Dean, Reginald
Dept. of Sustainability & Environment
de Souza, Roger
Doos, Chris
Drysdale, John
Dunne, Tyson
Elder, Janice
Fairfax Photos
Gerrard, Nannette
Grayden, Jess
Hamilton, Graham
Heinemann, Anthony
Help for Wildlife - Denise Garratt
Herwijnen Photography
Hill, Bill
Horsham Golf Club

Hull, Darryl
Iarai, Tony
Jones, Mark
Jowett, Erin
Jowett, Leigh
Kemezys, Paul
King, Leslie
Kinglake Historical Society
Kleinig, Andrew
Knight, Mark
Knudsen, Ross
Lackas, Sandra
Langmead, Fern
Lay, Rodney
Lloyd, Adrian
Lynn, Jason & Ruth
Mapley, Barry
Marysville Historic Society
Marysville Tourism Society
McMeikin, Peter
Mountain Monthly
NewsPix
Newstead, Mick
Nicholls, David
Nixon, Christine – c/o Victorian Bushfire Reconstruction Authority
NSW Rural Fire Service
O'Toole, Sean
Page, Neil
Pakenham, Keith
Pearson, Ian & Jacqui
Picture Media
Police Dog Squad
Quinn, Shane
Rooftop Maps – Robin Rishworth
Red Cross - Rodney Dekker
Redden, Carol
Roche, Chris
Rice, Peter
Smith, Peter
State Emergency Services (SES)
Stevenson, Simon
Sykes, Don
The Building Commission
The Salvation Army
The Herald and Weekly Times Photographic Collection (HWT)
Thornton, Rohan
Tolhurst, Dr Kevin
Tree, David
Wienroider, Barry
Wigginton, Gavin
Wright, Andrew
Victorian Police

Our thanks goes to countless other individuals and organisations who assisted with the book and to those who may have submitted material and photographs which was not printed in Firestorm.